111 DAYS OF A MOUNTAIN FLOWER

ACHALA BHAT

INDIA · SINGAPORE · MALAYSIA

ISBN
Paperback 979-8-89777-384-8
Hardcase 979-8-89961-804-8

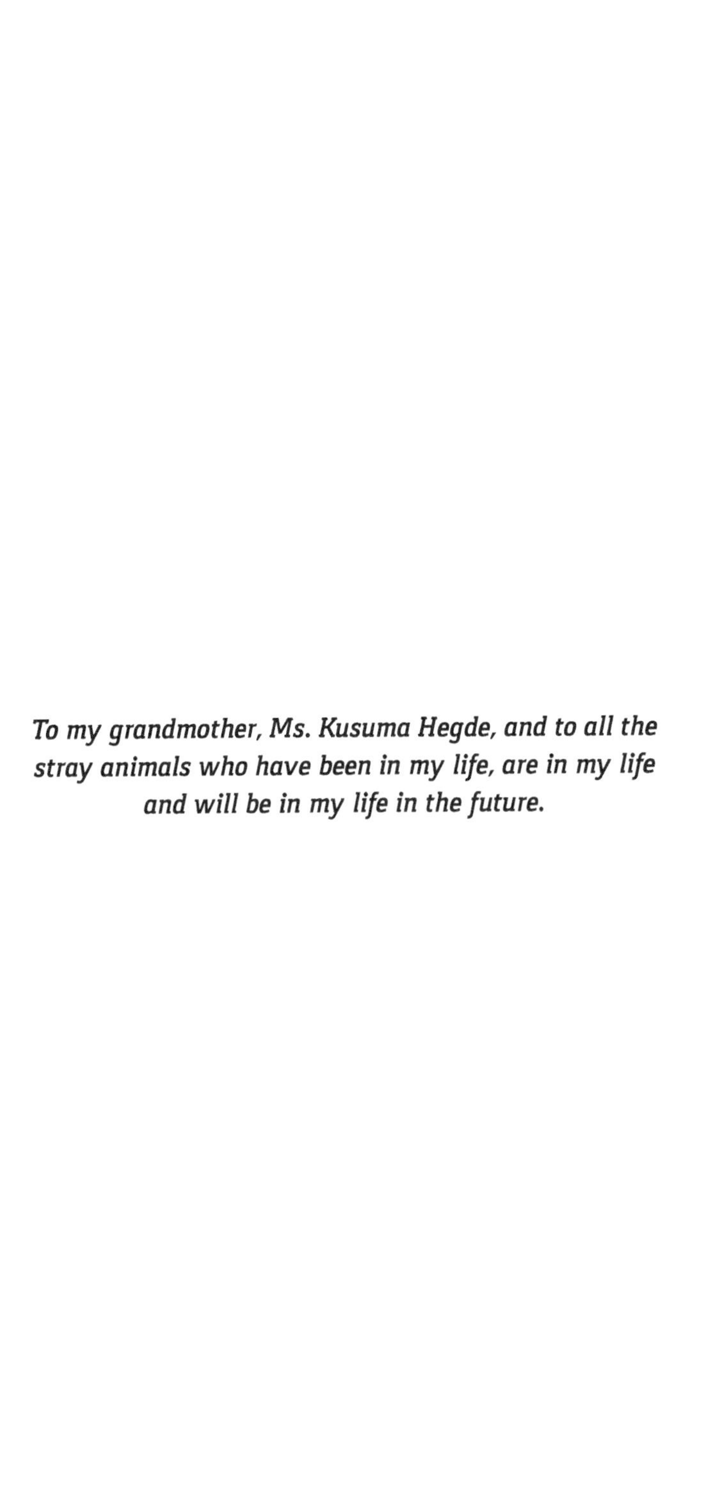

To my grandmother, Ms. Kusuma Hegde, and to all the stray animals who have been in my life, are in my life and will be in my life in the future.

CONTENTS

Contents

Contents

Introduction and Context

This book is an account of my days spent in a gorgeous and one-of-a-kind penthouse I lived in. It was a rented place, and when I moved in, I had survived and thrived more than a few bad years. This house gave me a reason to live, breathe more, and believe in good things happening to us in unexpected ways. I have documented 111 days of stay here. What I do for work, what happens at work, and other personal events have been intentionally kept out of the documents, as that dilutes the purpose of the book, which is to enjoy and celebrate the mundane and little things of life.

I had named my house "Bettada Hoovu", which means "flower of the mountain" in my mother tongue, Kannada (a language spoken in Southern India in the state of Karnataka). This was also the name of a popular Kannada movie of the 70s. I chose this name because this flat was a penthouse, providing a beautiful view of Bangalore. I moved here in June 2024, when the world was rife with wars, hatred, political divide, event-based view of life, and much more, but something as beautiful as this house happened to me. Social media is at its peak, and most humans post about the "events" and "milestones" in their lives, completely overlooking the beauty of the little things around us, daily.

This book is an attempt to contribute to the genre of "slice of life", which is not very prominent in India, by showcasing to the reader the joy of little things that often go unnoticed. It is also an attempt to address the falling social health, especially in my city of Bangalore, where most people live alone, away from their families, and to convey to the reader that they can still find joy in solitude. I hope you feel seen through my journey.

DAY 1 - 19/7/2024

THE DAY I BEFRIENDED JIMMI

I began my day working from home and was already excited about getting my terrace space cleaned and having the coffee by myself. Despite the very evident disinterest by the maid, my terrace is SO much cleaner now, and it already feels good. My coffee today was perfect. The colour, the texture, everything. I had my coffee by myself and kept my phone away as well. A ritual I have promised myself. I was not very motivated to go for my workouts today, but I did. I am glad and proud of that.

On my way back, I befriended a new furry friend, and I plan to name him Jimmi. I fed him 6 biscuits and he was very happy to eat them. It's funny, those biscuits have been in my bag for months, and I noticed them only a few days back. Looks like his name was written on them, and he was destined to eat them. I am happy I made a new friend. The walk from the gym to Bettada Hoovu was pleasant as always. The fragrance of the flowers and a glimpse of *Beasty* * (although she didn't notice me), made it richer.

I ended the day with some journaling, treated myself to some good music, and received a fresh set of laundry, as though it were the icing on the cake. Today was also the day I journaled this sitting on the terrace. It feels good! But maybe it will get better when my sore shoulders from today's workouts have healed a bit more.:P

---

* Beasty - A black Labrador dog in the locality, who often greets me on my way to the gym and is my best friend.

DAY 2 - 20/7/2024

THE DAY I APPRECIATED THE EAGLES

A slow day today. Intentionally so. I read about 20 pages of my current book, The Island of Missing Trees by Elif Shafak, first thing in the morning. My cook cooked spicy *paneer* * with peas for both lunch and dinner today, and a strong *Filter coffee* * to start the day. Coffee, of course, I brewed myself. I forgot to mention yesterday that the most important thing I have thanks to Bettada Hoovu is the view of eagles flying and whistling loudly. It tells me to keep my view high, fly bravely through it, and whistle loudly, nevertheless, and proclaim the platform you are on - that is the highest. It tells me not to lower my vision and never apologise for taking a higher ground on things. I watched them as I sipped my coffee today

---

* Goa - A small state on the western coast of India, known for its nature, scenic beaches, and party life. A popular tourist destination.

* Urban Company - An app-based home service offering, headquartered in India

and then retired indoors to take a workshop on managing weight plateau. The workshop turned out to be more valuable than envisioned. The trainer was pretty cool and also knowledgeable about the topic. I learnt a thing or 2 about my own body and also more about certain nuances of a healthy lifestyle.

I enjoyed the spicy paneer for lunch and then took a much-needed nap for an hour. This was followed by a self-pampering grooming session by my favourite lady from *Urban Company* *. She was elated to see that I had now moved to a better-looking flat and that I had kept my loyalty to her service. I also spent some time checking the cyclone movements at *Goa* *, where I will visit next Friday. Not that the rains scare me, but cyclones do. The day ended with me buying chamomile tea at a discounted rate from *Swiggy Instamart* *, and those who have consumed it earlier know that it's a bit of a cost for those tea bags. Well, at least in India.

The rain was completely gone today. It felt good, and moreover, it felt even better to see the sun after 5 days! The sight of the clouds racing away into the horizon is a treat in the night sky. Maybe that implies I will see better days ahead, and all my life's seeming "clouds" have faded away.

---

* Swiggy Instamart - The instant grocery delivery offering of Swiggy, an Indian food ordering and delivery company

* Filter Coffee - A strong coffee, akin to but stronger than Cappuccino, made in Southern India

* Paneer - Cottage Cheese

DAY 3 - 22/7/2024

THE DAY I DECIDED TO BID GOODBYE TO MY SHAME

Began the day watching *HOTD* * E6, S2. It was lukewarm, to be honest. The storyline didn't seem to be developing well. I started for the office at 8:30 am, but I got an auto and reached the office on time.

Small joys. It is sunny again now, after gloomy and rainy weather for the last full week. I have also been binge-watching Pachinko *, S1, thanks to a kind friend who shared his Apple TV+ credentials. Lucky to have met good people in the past. Work was swift today. I took 3 to 4 rounds of the campus, which was very rejuvenating, and had a good chat with a colleague with whom I seem to connect reasonably well. I got home and swept my flat with the vacuum robot. I felt good after cleaning, and then I took a small nap. I was contemplating bunking my

---

* HOTD - Abbreviation for "House of the Dragon", a popular fantasy series on HBO

* Pachinko - A popular American television show on Apple TV, based on the novel of the same name by Min Jin Lee

dance class but went for it nevertheless. I was still sure of walking out in the 2nd half of it, but stayed through the entire class, and more so, even enjoyed it.

I greeted my cat *Puff* * on the video call, and every time I see him, I feel like he is the marvel of the universe. Maybe that's how all mothers feel about their children. I also received a video of my performance yesterday and uploaded it with a bit of courage. Somehow, I have never liked looking at myself speaking. A sense of disgust comes up, though I am a well-known speaker in the *Toastmasters* * circle and also an appreciated performer. I plan to get over this self-shame, this year. Winding down this day with more Pachinko and then a bit of the book, Island of Missing Trees by Elif Shafak.

---

*   Puff - Name of my pet cat

*   Toastmasters - A 100+-year-old LA-based non-profit educational organisation helping members build public speaking and leadership skills, with clubs across the globe

DAY 4 - 24/7/2024

THE DAY I NAMED THE "VICTORY STREET"

Phew. I had a jammed day at work. The morning began on a sour note when my cook misplaced the lid on the jar of my mixer, which led to all the *chutney* * getting sprayed throughout my hall. It was a disgusting sight, and her regretful, yet unapologetic smile at the end of the act made me detest her a bit. I did not express my anger in words, though. What was done was done, and now had to be just cleaned out. I felt sorry for my dear Bettada Hoovu. I also feel glad that now I feel such a sense of belonging to my home that I was feeling sorry for it. I promise to be very protective of it always.

Post work, I did an upper body workout after really grilling myself well at the gym for the past 2 days. Felt proud of myself. The class audience today was a bit warm, thankfully. On my way back, on the usual way where

---

*   Chutney - An Indian condiment made of mashed vegetables/fruits with spices and herbs, with some seasoning

Beasty resides, a thought came to my mind that I should rename it "Victory Street". Because I have literally been slaying at every class, and my personality has blossomed into a more sociable person over the past year. I got back, worked a bit, and then did some packing to head home tomorrow. I will go to Goa for the next 4 days after that. This time, I will be looking at this time off with ease. No mindless café hopping. But nevertheless, I'm looking forward to visiting North Goa after 2 years. This was the place that held me during my birthday in 2017 when I was a broken soul. It taught me that there is space and place for everyone, and with the right time off, anyone can pick themselves up.

DAY 5 - 30/7/2024

THE DAY I RELISHED SLOW BURN IN LIFE

I returned to Bettada Hoovu today, after my mini vacation in Goa. While I initially dreaded taking the vacation, I am glad I took it. Life is too short to postpone vacations and the much-needed off-time. It took about 5-7 minutes to restore my abode back to normal, and it felt amazing. I cancelled my dance class and opted for yoga instead. Again, a right decision. It was a slow day, and thankfully, that helped me recover from my vacation lag. Yeah, that's a term I use for the lag you have to return to real life after a vacation. I was also tired from the trip to the airport yesterday. After my yoga session, I felt quite refreshed and truly felt like the freshness of the trip had settled in.

The highlight of the day was reading 40 pages of my current book - Island of Missing Trees, out on the terrace area, watching the rain. What I love about Bettada Hoovu is its views. I saw the rain travelling along with its source clouds, and this is the closest I have seen rainfall. It rained quite heavily, with strong winds blowing, but watching it from Bettada Hoovu gave me a sense of safety and an opportunity to admire nature's fury (or maybe beauty?). The book was no less. It starts slow, every time I start reading it, and then slowly you don't realise when you've been swept off by its tornado of beautiful metaphors, only to arrive at a shore far away from where you started reading it for the day. Slow burn is the theme of this year, maybe. I watched *K-drama* * a bit, made some veggies, and resigned for the day, with this journal being the last activity of the day. Another beautiful day at Bettada Hoovu.

---

*   K-drama - The dramas produced and directed in South Korea

DAY 6 - 31/7/2024

THE DAY I SAW BOTH APATHY AND KINDNESS

The day began completely fresh after a good rest yesterday. My cook/maid got the right mix for Upma, and I relished it. She also requested me to put in a word for more jobs for her, because apparently some highly privileged peeps of *HSR Layout* * laid her off after she was away for 3 weeks owing to Dengue. It's funny how people don't want to do their household chores even if it is for 3 weeks, and even if it means that it keeps their home happier, cleaner, and healthier.

I was also unpleasantly amused at how unkindness takes over some people in others' times of need. I immediately took to circulating her number to relevant people in hopes of a good job opportunity for her. She also requested part-time jobs for her children, who are studying, yet have to take up some work to bring food to their table. My life was very privileged, I surmised.

---

* HSR Layout - Hosur, Sarjapura Road Layout, a prominent suburb in the southeastern part of Bangalore, where I lived.

I went to the office today and loved the cosy weather. I sipped some black coffee whose flavours melted in my mouth, and I sipped them very slowly and carefully. I also enquired about the health of another colleague who was also affected by Dengue, and an exchange about how gruesome a hospital stay is. This is all we need as humans, I feel. An honest conversation. With anyone, literally. Sometimes we just want to be heard and seen, nothing more. Riches don't matter, nor their past, their beauty, or even their acquaintance.

I got back home and hit my workouts and did fabulously well there. I called my grandmother to check on the rains, to see if she was keeping sane in them, and, more importantly, to see if there was enough food stocked up. Surprisingly, she seemed more jovial than I had imagined her to be. She also told me that the rain had reduced there that day. Wow. Sometimes things don't turn out like the worst-case scenarios we imagine. I was glad to know that, and also the fact that there were some working staff on our farm who were helping her out. The world is still sane and kind, I mused. The day began on a note of unkindness and ended with a note of kindness. I love it!

DAY 7 - 1/8/2024

The Day I Learnt About Human Impact and My Own

The day began with a spicy aloo matar sabji made by my cook, which funnily took her an hour to do. This day turned out much brighter. I was very tired to go to the gym, but I made it and worked out at 60% capacity. When I got back home, I had a call with one of my coachee, who I was coaching to enter back into the workforce in an HR role. I still remember my first conversation with her. It was Jan 30, one of the worst days in 2024 for me, and I had just cried out for 30 minutes to my mom and mentioned clearly that I wanted to give up on life.

I had just wiped my tears to look a bit sane on my call with her and logged in with messy hair and a disoriented expression. She was a live wire filled with enthusiasm and ambition, and I immediately shifted my focus from my sorrow to her story and aspirations. We quickly carved out a career map and were regularly in touch via coaching sessions. Fast-forward to March, she completed the training I had recommended and became market-ready.

Fast-forward to May, and she landed a job with a great role.

Firstly, this makes me aware of the impact I can create, however tiny. I was questioned on why I was worthy of coaching people, and I kept going, ignoring all those comments. It paid off. I made an impact bigger than every naysayer whatsoever. Most important of all, I pumped one woman back into the workforce of India, a country with one of the world's lowest rates of female workforce participation. Even on your worst day, you carry immense potential. The world around you carries immense potential; just go and show up.

I also got in touch with an ex-colleague and chatted over a perspective for 30 minutes. Unfortunately, or fortunately, I learnt about his impressive journey of beating the odds of financial crunch and studying and then succeeding, only now - that is, a year after I left my last firm where he was my colleague. Nevertheless, I was glad we could reconnect and have a candid chat, share perspectives, and joke a bit. Human connections are GOLD.

DAY 8 - 2/8/2024

THE DAY NATURE WON OVER "COOLNESS"

The day began with an earlier-than-usual trip to the office. When I got home, I was quite knackered and decided to cancel my dance class and resort to yoga for the day's workout. This opened sometime in the evening, and I chose to spend it in the terrace area, with a cup of filter coffee and the book I am currently reading. It was pleasant as always, until someone 2-3 buildings away started to sing loudly, with a guitar. Sure, they were not off note, but I have never understood the mindset of enjoying at the expense of others' disturbance. I was hoping to hear the birds chirp, the soft pitter-patter of the rain, the mellowed sound of the wind, but no. Someone wanted to sing loudly under the guise of "being cool". My discomfort here is a small matter. But there are many houses around with senior citizens, infants (there is a paediatric hospital!) or even someone who possibly has worked through the night shift and wants to earn their decent share of sleep for the day. Unfortunately, this is one thing I hate about HSR. Loud house parties with no remorse or civic sense under the guise of "Hey, we are enjoying and we are cool." Thankfully, the solo orchestra stopped after some time, and I could hear the cuckoo rejoicing in the weather and thanking me for thinking about them.

I also relished my yoga session today. I feel that if you are into fitness and workouts, you cannot skip a routine on building flexibility as a part of fitness. Pick yoga or pick Tai-chi, but build flexibility. Yoga is the only form of workout that acts on your vagus nerve and hence soothes your cortisol and stress levels. I feel this in every bone of mine whenever I practice yoga. After my yoga session, I spoke to my mom for an hour and then just relaxed for the rest of the day. I am proud that I chose yoga over cardio today, which is something my body really needed.

DAY 9 - 3/8/2024

THE DAY OF PERFECT FILTER COFFEE

The day began with some soreness from Thursday's workout still lingering. I decided to opt for a 30-minute Latino dance class instead of a 50-minute Zumba class, and it was worth it. I took an extra hour of nap and felt fresh after that. My protein shake and filter coffee were both perfect. Way to begin the weekend! The best part of the day was finding another spot to read on the terrace, reading 30 pages of this lovely book in the mild sun, and overhearing the chirps of the birds and occasional bell rings from the temple across the road. A beautiful morning.

In the afternoon, I drove about 5 km (which was quite taxing in the traffic!) to purchase some recreational items for my home. I made that decision impulsively and felt that sometimes it's okay to make even uncalculated decisions. I got back home after that and took a mini-nap at around 6:30 pm. I ended the day with some mild music, journaling, and building a night ritual for myself.

I watched a random tarot reading video for my sign that spoke some relevant things. What it said was that I should change my approach to things, use my logic and wisdom, and find different ways to get what I want. Anyway, despite everything, I feel I will get what I want because that's what has always happened in my life. I fall, collapse, get buried, sprout out, and then bloom - finally getting what I want. Cheers!

DAY 10 - 4/8/2024

THE DAY I GRIEVED, MADE SAUTEED MUSHROOMS FOR THE FIRST TIME, AND CELEBRATED FRIENDSHIP DAY!

The day began on a great note. I woke up at 7 am, feeling very fresh and ready for the day, though my alarm was for 8:35 am for a 10 am workout. I made myself a very fulfilling breakfast (2 protein breads and gunpowder made of flax seeds), and read a bit of the book on the terrace. The workout at 10 am was great as well. I could do pendlay rows after many days and nailed it in the ab workouts. The skies have cleared now, and I mused to myself that I would soon be able to go for walks in the parks nearby.

Sunday is also the cooking day! I cooked myself sauteed mushrooms and green peas, and it tasted heavenly, albeit too spicy. However, I was happy that I was able to stick to my cooking discipline and cook for myself independently.

I fell asleep to a nap thanks to the prevailing workout soreness. I woke up craving a ginger *chai* * and ordered it from *Chaayos* *.

I later went out on the terrace to complete the rest of the book, and I overheard a couple of women talking loudly about some cat and meow meow and something similar. That was enough for me to get intrigued and walk up to the terrace railings, where I saw 2 women in the building next to mine talking to a man with a bit of distress. I couldn't see any cat nearby, so I waited until the man moved a bit, and I could see a dead cat near his feet. This was a cat I had spotted twice in that building and nearby, and it felt like someone punched my stomach hard enough to make me faint. That is how I felt when my first pet, Amar (a ginger tabby cat), died, and all my other furry friends, namely, Coco, Socks, Diva, Tinkle, and Sugar (all Indie dogs), had died. I felt giddy and kept looking at the dead cat until my grief could resurface and then melted away.

Sadly, it's we humans who dominate the ecosystem of this planet and not the innocent animals. Every animal deserves to live, dream, and thrive like us, but they don't, and sadly, no one seems to find solutions for this or even be bothered by it. I returned to my terrace chair and tried calming my breath. I felt giddy for another 15 more minutes and then decided to resign to the order of things on this planet like I always do whenever I see or hear about an animal passing.

---

*   Chai - The milk-based tea made in India, with spices

*   Chaayos - A popular outlet headquartered in India for Chai

I also finished reading the book, The Island of Missing Trees, today. A marvel of a book. Highly recommend it. The day ended with meeting a friend of 14 years after 3 years. In this world of dwindling friendships (which is btw faster amongst female friendships), I am glad I have at least one friend who has lasted the duration and the strength. Both of us had a terrible last 3 years, and we were glad to see each other sane and alive on the other side. Also, not to mention, today was coincidentally Friendship Day! A very rich day, with a variety of emotions and activities.

DAY 11 - 5/8/2024

THE DAY I JUMPED A LOT IN DANCE CLASS

The day began on a sombre note when I watched the finale of House of the Dragon, and it was highly unsatisfactory. I despised the storyline, but fabulous acting as always by all the artists.

I got home from work at noon, with a bit of a sore throat, and rested like crazy. It was quite rewarding and I am grateful to my flat and the money that rents this flat for providing me with such a haven. It refreshed me enough to hit the dance workouts in the evening. It rained very heavily around 5 pm, and I was thanking the universe that the dead cat I mentioned in the last entry was taken away for cremation this morning. God bless the poor soul, and I prayed silently that it be born in the Netherlands, where I hear no stray animals are left, and freedom of being a human is paramount.

My dance workout was beyond good. It had been some time since I jumped as much as I did after my foot fracture, and I totally let myself loose and enjoyed the class today.

Great choice of songs by the trainer as well! That is what life is about, maybe - to push yourself to dance it out on bad days, for all you know, it might be worth it. I ended the day by speaking to my mother and 2 people from my circle, who were kind enough to listen to my ordeals at 9 in the night.

DAY 12 - 6/8/2024

THE DAY I APPRECIATED THE POWER OF ACQUAINTANCES

The day began on a hungry note, and I munched on some 99% dark chocolate that I had. I also got my terrace cleaned, which I have now aimed to do twice a month. My coffee tasted stronger, and I liked the kick of it. On days that are hazy, confusing, and upsetting, a strong coffee is all you need in the morning.

A kind colleague invited me to join her for lunch, and I was very glad she did. Not that I ever mind having lunch by myself, but I appreciate her gesture and her sensitivity towards me. I got home from a good yoga session. The highlight of the day truly was 3 of my acquaintances, one of them being an ex-manager, who took some time out to help me out in a dilemma situation. It just required one message from me to them, and they all jumped in to solve it for me. I am proud to have the rapport and power of my network, who are very genuine to me and my ambitions in life. There was another acquaintance who also guided me through the chat. Wow, and that makes it 4.

I also hit 250 weeks of consistency in my workouts at my gym, be it at their centre or on the app. That is like 5 years of consistently investing in fitness. That is the tenure assigned to elected governments in my country. I salute myself on this feat. This has involved meticulously planning my workout schedule, being excited about it genuinely, and showing up, come what may and wherever possible. During travels, visits to natives, homestays, beachside, deserts, anywhere.

The day ended with a coaching session with a girl from my alma mater, who was very impressive because of her grit, ambition, and sheer interest in doing better. She also mentioned that she wanted to get exposure to other cities in India, other than her own, via work, and that was something I always endorse since that has been my own journey and the one that was very rewarding. Happy to have the opportunity and stature to coach such women who also, in turn, reflect my passion for life.

DAY 13 - 7/8/2024

THE DAY I MET BOTH AN UNFRIENDLY HUMAN AND A FRIENDLY DOG

The day began on a busy note. I had to rush to work and then engage in back-to-back meetings. I had my coffee with 4 lovely colleagues, and it was good to have company.

I got home to my new phone. I have used my old phone VERY extensively since 2021, and it's since then that my life has become extremely difficult, grievous, and challenging. It stayed by me through all of it and still functions decently well. I could see myself on that phone (or maybe the other way around?). Both of us went through things unimaginably difficult and came out alive and thriving and still functioning decently well on the other side. I saluted my phone and kissed it thank you, before packing it safely inside my cupboard. I am also grateful that I now have a job that pays me enough to buy a good phone without an EMI.

I went to work out after setting up my phone and was a bit low on energy there. Nevertheless, I gave my best. My gym peeps have been running partner-ab workouts for this whole week to celebrate Friendship Day and today, too, we had a partner-ab challenge. I looked at the very fit lady standing next to me, and she couldn't be bothered less. She turned her face away and chose to do the workout alone, implicitly, I had to as well, as the rest of the class was paired. I looked at her again in the second round, but she turned her face away again. The state of social health in Bangalore is damaged beyond repair, I mused to myself. We all need to believe people around us and be just normally human with them, at the very least. I was not hurt much, I have been there myself in 2017-18.

I headed back after the gym via the road where Beasty resides, and voila! She was sitting outside the house! I saw a couple patting her and asking her to join them before leaving her to greet me. The way everyone trusts Beasty is synonymous with how she trusts others, too. She sat by me for a good 7 minutes, and I took some selfies with her, as a token of Friendship Day. She is my bestesssttt friend in all HSR Layout, after all. The day ended with a bit of soreness in my muscles, and another day of feeling low, albeit made better by Beasty's presence!

DAY 14 - 8/8/2024

THE DAY I REALISED THE TRUE MEANING OF GOOD LUCK

The day is triple 8! Lionsgate portal of luck, apparently. I began my day with an informal chat with my cook, which does not happen often. The day was relaxing, and the workload wasn't much for the day. I also caught up a bit on my K-drama, Crash Landing on You, the one I am watching right now. This art form of K-drama has kept me sane and hopeful since December 2022, when I started watching it. I also ordered a delicious hot chocolate for myself after many days, and sipped it on the terrace, with the rain, floating clouds, and an eagle giving me company.

I also discovered today that many fighter jets fly over my apartment in the evening, and I could see most of them very clearly. One of them flew scarily low, and I was marvelled by its sight. The sight of that fighter jet flying so formidably taught me to fly high and strong, always. There will be many who cannot fly to our level, who might pass comments, be naysayers, and not believe in our dreams, but we need to be that fighter jet and fly its flight without giving a single care about them. I also walked in my terrace area for 30 minutes today, and it felt amazing. I ordered food for dinner today and signed off my day with 2 cups of chamomile tea.

Maybe that portal of luck did open today, because I felt very positive and hopeful today, without any significant reason for it, and that is what abundance is about.

DAY 15 - 11/8/2024

THE DAY A PORTAL OPENED TO A BEAUTIFUL FANTASY

Spent only the evening onwards at Bettada Hoovu. Today, when I was riding back in the cab from my parents' place to Bettada Hoovu, it was by far the most optimistic ride. The road was the same, the travel mode was the same (car/cab), as was the destination.

What seemed different were the skies. Bangalore skies are known to be beautiful, and I regret that most people choose to focus on the traffic they are stuck in and not on the skies, which constantly showcase the designs and splendour of different shapes of clouds. Today, the skies were clear and had different colours in them, and it made me feel lighter on emotions. It felt possible—everything, every dream.

Throughout the 75 minutes of the ride, I had someone on my mind. He is seas away, someone not of my race, someone who doesn't speak my language, and someone I have never met. And yet he was on my mind. Though he is my celebrity crush, I felt glad that my mind could make some space for him for 75 minutes on a day when I felt terribly lonely.

That's the beauty of life. There is still a lot to explore, lots to do, many people to meet, and many more memories to make. Upon reaching Bettada Hoovu, as I write this, I see crackers sparkling in the sky, as though they applaud what I just wrote here. Who knows, maybe he, too, is watching these crackers 7 seas away, and a portal might open through which I can travel to him.

I ended the day with a movie night on the terrace. World-class happiness!

DAY 16 - 12/8/2024

THE DAY I MET A METAPHORIC K-DRAMA HERO

It rained BAD last night. For a while, I thought the water would seep into my windows on the fifth floor. It rained all night, and when I woke up, the terrace area, including the covered area, was completely drenched. I displaced some items of immediate use with compassion towards them and towards the rain that drenched them. I started to wonder how unpredictable the weather and my journal entries are.

Just yesterday (last entry), I mentioned clear skies (and they were indeed clear), and the reader might just immediately wonder which section was a lie from me. I assure you, dear reader, that both were true accounts, and it is the erratic Bangalore weather that humbles us every now and then. I was all ready to leave for the office when I came across the news that all the exit points from the HSR Layout, where I stay, were submerged and cabs and autos would be inaccessible for some time.

I made myself filter coffee, and when I set out to the terrace area to enjoy it, nature proved me wrong again. The sun shone brightly in the east, piercing sharply through the dark clouds. This was enough to make me smile and enjoy the company of Mr. Sun and my filter coffee for the morning. The day was relaxing, and I could get a good workout session as well.

When I returned, I watched a very engaging episode of K-drama and cried to my content. Today was a beautiful day, and the highlight of the day was indeed Mr. Sun, who sure made an entry like the male leads of K-dramas who pop out of nowhere to save their woman (usually with an umbrella in sudden rains)!.

DAY 17 - 13/8/2024

THE DAY I FELL A PREY TO THE SECOND MALE LEADS

I have been waking up to the sun cracking through dark clouds every day. What a signal from the universe. I always smile whenever I see sight.

I got home about 30 minutes early from the office so that I could hit my dance class. Amping up my fitness routine a bit to earn my *Biscuit Rottis* * at *Mangalore* * next weekend. Almost finished my K-drama today, and once again, for the third consecutive time, I loved the romance of the second leads more than the main leads. It also made me realise something about my own choices. The second leads, especially the second male leads in all

---

*　Mangalore - A city on the western coast of India, known for its pristine beaches, educational institutions, and for being an industrial port city

*　Biscuit Rotti - A fried snack made of wheat or maize flour with a filling of grated coconut and steamed legumes with some seasoning and spices. Made in cities on the west coast of India, in the state of Karnataka, in Southern India

these 3 dramas, were imperfect, and made horrible choices in their past, but eventually came around for the women they loved. I'm not sure if it's my choice or just the bait of the writer, to which I have fallen prey!

I wrote my entry today in the terrace area, and the wind is quite sinister here. By sinister, I mean, awkwardly good enough to make you not want to go inside.

DAY 18 - 14/8/2024

THE DAY I REALISED THE PRIVILEGE OF HAVING A LIFT IN MY APARTMENT

Would you believe me if I said last year, this day, and the year before, this day, I was in one of my worst phases? I wouldn't believe that myself, but this morning when I woke up, I realised that. So, dear reader, I want to tell you that things do get better. You will feel better, and such is the cycle of life that everything is temporary - including what you are going through. Having said that, I felt a bit sick and hence opted to work from home and spent most of the day just resting, drinking fluids, and sleeping. In fact, I even considered cancelling my workouts. Thankfully, I made it to the lighter version of the workouts by 5 pm, and I was glad I could make it. I met Beasty today, again, and today she could recognise me from a distance. Very few joys in the world are more precious than someone feeling happy at the sight of you. Beasty gave me that joy today.

While walking back from the gym, I wondered if I would have anything for a journal entry today. Since I was only resting, sleeping, and occasionally working. I went to the extent of thinking if there would be more such days and if I would ever complete my book. But when I reached my apartment and found the lift to have stopped working temporarily, I realised that I still had some privileges in life that I was taking for granted. Like the lift! I had to climb up to the fifth floor AFTER a workout session. I ordered some snacks for myself, and while they arrived, I also wrote a poem. At night, I connected with the Toastmasters (public speakers) fraternity of Toronto, and they have become like family for a year or so now. A very optimal effect of the pandemic. Seamless connections across borders.

I mused to myself to never underestimate any day, even if I fall sick. Because every breath we take is a dream to most others who lived on this planet. (18)

DAY 19 - 15/8/2024

THE DAY I SPOKE CALMED MY RAGE WITH GRATITUDE

A short day at Bettada Hoovu as I head elsewhere at noon. I started the day slow and then decided to go for a leg day at the gym, to cool off the rage in my heart owing to the recent rape and brutal murder in my country, which ironically coincides with Independence Day, today. The workout helped. I could lift my PR with ease, and with each lift, my body screamed, "Thank you!"

I got back home and rewarded myself with a filter coffee for living up to the commitment I had made to myself this week, in terms of fitness. A massive rage screams in my heart, nevertheless. I have been silenced, asked to change, feel guilty for who I am, and a lot more, in my country. Of course, they might happen in other countries too, but my countrymen don't even guarantee my safety. I tell myself to mellow my rage down (like always), to close the entry for today, feeling grateful that I am safe and alive today.

DAY 20 - 18/8/2024

THE DAY OF KINDNESS AND PRAYERS

It's ironic (and eerie) that what I want to write today is a continuation of the last entry. Last week, I got in touch with a gentleman from Singapore who helped me find a Toastmasters club there and ensured a grand welcome there. His kindness and energy were obvious. Unfortunately, today I learnt that he has passed away. I might have been the last person he got acquainted with, the last person he added on FB, and the last person he was kind to. In the very interaction with him, he taught me to be kind to everyone every day, every time. We never know what tomorrow has in store for us.

I returned to Bettada Hoovu last evening and made some *Masala Makhana* * for myself. Felt good to cook some snacks for myself, which will now last the whole week. I ended the day with a bit of K-drama, detox tea, and watching some fireworks from the terrace. (20)

---

*   Masala Makhana - Makhana translates to fox nuts or lotus seeds, which are eaten as a form of snack in India, either raw, salted or with spices (masala)

DAY 21 - 19/8/2024

THE DAY MY UNIVERSE FELT BOUNTIFUL

"Envision, create, and believe in your own universe, and the universe will form around you."

A line from the book I am currently reading, Delivering Happiness by Tony Hsieh. I felt validated when I read it. By these notes and investing in enriching my Bettada Hoovu, I am doing precisely that! This piece of my universe might be unconventional and little, but it is very significant to me and I am confident it will lead to a better life that is to come. Our lives don't get covered by the press, and some of us may not even have a social media presence but believe in your universe. It is beautiful in its own way, and you will find a tribe who would want to be a part of it if not today.

My day started very well, and I made myself a good bowl of protein shake. I also prayed today and felt grounded after that. This was followed by a relaxed day at work and a very elaborate reading session in the terrace area. Felt refreshed after that. As though this wasn't enough, I had a great dance class as well at the gym. Bountiful, that's the word for today at Bettada Hoovu.

55

DAY 22 - 20/8/2024

THE DAY I HAD A DATE WITH THE FULL MOON

Gah, a difficult day. I had to visit the doctor due to flu-like symptoms and change my workouts to a brisk walk in the park. Well, I thoroughly enjoyed the latter. The meds worked, and I started to feel better by night. I was feeling very lonely, thanks to the plight of dealing with illnesses alone, and that's when Mr. Full Moon decided to give me company for dinner. I had a very romantic dinner by the moonlight of the full moon, and I heard the melodious chants from a nearby temple.

Pause, look around, and you will never feel lonely like they say. I also captured the very first full moon picture from Bettada Hoovu. Many more to come, and looking forward to a day filled with opportunities and better health. I thank my country for its abundant, easily accessible, and economically available medical facilities. (22)

DAY 23 - 21/8/2024

The Day I Had My 2nd Date with the Full Moon

I write this, witnessing the moon right in front of me in all its glory. Bettada Hoovu has given me so many beautiful moments like this that they now are more than the number of beautiful moments I have had in the past 2 years put together. This is now my most favourite part of the day, when I write about my time at Bettada Hoovu, with the wind, moon, and hustling trees as my witnesses. Nature is always with us, yet we say we are lonely. Not fair.

Given that I am still sick, my workout today was just circling and walking around in the terrace area of Bettada Hoovu, which turned out very effective. I took the time to rest, and I feel I should be completely fine by tomorrow. I was also very excited to plan and look forward to my visit to Mangalore, the coming weekend. Mangalore is where I spent the 5 best months of my life (of my life as of this date when I write this. I hope I have more such happy phases in life.) and where I first embarked on the journey of my dark night, which I sometimes feel hasn't ended yet. But maybe, this weekend when I visit, it will come to an end. Or maybe, I will find some answer, just like the protagonist of the book "The Alchemist" did, just before finding the treasure. Nevertheless, my excitement stays the same. Closing this day with some humorous K-drama time.

DAY 24 - 22/8/2024

The Day I Was Busy to Heal

It seemed like overindulgence in the cold winds of the night, watching the blue moon, and it worsened my cold and flu. But it's not just the outdoors that's beautiful at Bettada Hoovu. It's also the comfort of the bed and the shelter it provides. The day was very busy, resting. Often, when people say they are busy, they mention work or an activity of some kind. But I have always believed that even resting needs to be made time for, and you can always be busy resting as well.

I closed the day with roti and my favourite *Rajma* *, as I head to Mangalore tomorrow and have an early flight to catch.

---

*   Rajma - A spicy curry made of red kidney beans, prominently made in northern India

DAY 25 - 26/8/2024

THE DAY I MADE HARD DECISIONS, EASILY

Took some time out to recover from my flu and make some hard decisions in life. But I had a very strong support system to get me through both. It was my favourite city of Mangalore, its extremely kind people, its food, the sea breeze, some friends who are still there for me, some new ones made, and a nostalgic event. Wow, now that I've listed them all, I feel it's longer than I imagined it to be! Life is never easy, but with beautiful things, places, and people, we can all make it through.

I am writing this from my hall area because I am still too weak to sit in the terrace area and strain my lungs. I made masala makhana today, and that was very satisfying. I figured ordering that online would take 5-7 minutes for the delivery, and so would preparing it at home. But I went for a dance workout today and did reasonably well. Our body always vouches for us, only if we respect it. The way to my gym is a bit dark, and even a stare for more than 5 seconds from anyone who identifies as male can feel intimidating. I felt the same today. Planning to take the longer route out for my safety because the society here may not change before I die, but my safety needs to be preserved.

Nevertheless, returning to Bettada Hoovu always makes me feel I am loved and secure. I had a good vegetable mix for dinner and am looking forward to tomorrow for another day of much-needed rest. Also, I just completed a quarter of the century with these entries!

THE DAY I DISCOVERED A NEW WAY OF VALIDATION

A long day today. But I started it on a very good note with a brisk walk workout at my favourite park nearby. On my way to the park, my Bluetooth earphones died off their battery and I had 2 choices: walk back to Bettada Hoovu, charge them and then go to the park OR just go to the park and walk without earphones. I chose the latter.

The first 5 minutes felt a bit out of place, but then I eased into it. My inner voice, the sound of the birds, the excitement of the kids in the park, the raging vehicles rushing to work - everything felt like a song with a story, and I was able to complete a good number of steps in 30 minutes.

A lot of times, we look for external confirmation that we are indeed on the right track, that we are indeed doing good, that we are indeed making the right decision, and so on. When we don't find that external voice, we get disappointed. Or maybe scroll endlessly on social media for some random reels or a post to confirm it for us. Some of us even go to fortune tellers. Or look at our palm lines, keenly. But the real confirmation comes from within, dear friend. It's the inner voice you possibly suppressed, wondering if you were thinking too much. It's your own wisdom and experiences that you need to listen to for any confirmation of your potential and assured good times in the future.

I had a *kadak chai* * in the evening with the cold winds, with an eagle, a parrot, and 2 mynas that sat near me briefly. I also had a coaching session with an aspiring young lady, which I always enjoy. While I was closing the day and writing this write-up, I started to hear strange noises in the hall area, like- tic - tic - tic - tic - tic, at a steady pace. I thought the culprit was a lizard that had sneaked in accidentally from the terrace area, but it turned out to be the chickpeas I had kept for an overnight soak. I had a good laugh about my ignorance and apologised to Mr/Ms Lizard. I smiled at those chickpeas, pleading for it to turn into delicious *chole* * tomorrow.

---

*   Kadak Chai - A strong milky tea

*   Chole - A spicy curry made of chickpeas, mainly in northern India

DAY 27 - 29/8/2024

THE DAY I RETREATED, TO RELIVE

I woke up to a slow-paced day, and I enjoyed it. My cook makes excellent *Pongal* *, and I asked her to prepare it in a way that it would last me for both meals. I relished it both times and loved the rains that smashed Bangalore City around late noon. I made it to the gym and did some heavy back workouts while it was still raining outside. The day got cold with the rains, and then suddenly it didn't seem much at ease, because my lungs had yet to heal from the deadly viral flu I contracted last week.

Nevertheless, I took a walk in the terrace area at night and it made me feel at peace, thanks to the clouds that seemed to be marching away in the sky and the lights from a nearby rooftop café. I ended the day a bit tired, yet feeling grateful, as I had coached 3 aspiring women leaders this week. I am glad I can make a difference to India's terrible representation of women in the workforce.

---

* Pongal - A traditional dish prominently made in South India, from rice and pulses

DAY 28 - 30/8/2024

THE DAY I 1ST MET STREETIE LOVERS IN MY LANE

The day of assured salary - a luxury I did not have for the first few months of this year. Today is that day, and I am grateful for it. Today was also a day filled with many opportunities, very happy but challenging ones. I enjoyed my breakfast and coffee in the sun that came up today after an entire day of clouds and rain yesterday. Nature cares for us, I always feel. Evening seemed to have approached fast, and I practised yoga for the evening.

I also have good news to share. The black Indie dog on my lane, whom I presumed was lost, seems to be well cared for. He safely sits in front of a house, and I have seen one or 2 people patting him affectionately. God bless them, and I pray my Indie boy stays safe.

I had planned to eat outside for dinner today, and I did. Nepali food at Lama café. Trivia about Lama café is that it started its operations at HSR around the same time I moved to HSR. I am always happy to see the café doing well, because I think I have done well here too, and it is

a success story for both of us. I relished *Kothey momos* *
and *Thenthuk* * and then drove down for a petrol refill.
The drive from the petrol station was a bit long, and I
intentionally drove as slowly as I could to enjoy to chilled
winds and the glimmers of the hustle and bustle of HSR.

---

*   Kothey Momos - Nepalese pan-fried dumplings filled with
     either vegetable or meat

*   Thenthuk - A Tibetan hand-pulled noodle soup made of
     wheat flour dough and vegetable/meat

DAY 29 - 1/9/2024

The Day I Met Mona After a Long Time and Updated My Blackboard for 1st Time

It's my birthday month! September, for me, has always marked the beginning of something good and, most times, yielded very beautiful memories. That's also partly because I always ensure to plan my birthday in advance and celebrate my birth with all the galore it deserves. More on that later in the month.

I had a very beautiful day today, most of which was spent at my parents' place and quality time with my furry family. The day's highlight was meeting my best friend Mona, the cow. I was surprised that she still remembered me and devoured almost all the vegetables we had in our fridge. Mona is very special to me, and I felt very loved after meeting her today.

Once I reached Bettada Hoovu, I got a call from my grandmother, which was just what I needed that day. Sometimes, we don't realise that even though it may seem lonely and even though we may be distant from our loved ones, we are truly loved and never alone. Today was one such day when I was reminded of that. I updated the weekly blackboard at Bettada Hoovu (new home decor!) and made some masala makhana for the rest of the week, before retiring for the day.

DAY 30 - 2/9/2024

THE DAY I DISCOVERED THE ABUNDANCE OF HEALTHCARE NEAR ME

My breathing issues continue this week. On the night of 1st September, they almost choked me. I went to the office the next day, only to return early and head to a pulmonologist near Bettada Hoovu. When I was looking for a pulmonologist, I discovered that there were 2 top-rated ones within a radius of 1 km around Bettada Hoovu, as was the case with many other specialist doctors. I thanked my stars and felt grateful to live in an area with such amenities. Ease of medical care is never to be underestimated. To make this better, the doctor had a very offbeat approach to medicine and even assured me that he wouldn't leave the clinic until he saw me when I had called him for an appointment. Kind gestures, especially by doctors, go a long way.

I returned home, treated myself to a lemongrass tea, and slipped into a deep sleep, given the long day. What a luxury it is to get deep sleep!

DAY 31 - 4/9/2024

THE DAY HUMAN CONNECTION SAVED ME

The day began on a slow note, with me still reeling with flu-induced high heart rate. I asked my cook to make some pulao for both lunch and dinner and took a WFH to cater to my health. Around the afternoon, I was feeling very depressed owing to the turbulent last 2 years and its memories and I called up my mom to speak to her. Such is the beauty of human connection - the issue per se might not be solved, but when shared, it makes it so much lighter. Post this conversation, my day started to look better.

I sat on the terrace area and made myself a hot chocolate, around 5 pm. The initial idea was to drive to an aesthetic café near Bettada Hoovu and sip on some hot chocolate, but the view from the terrace area beat all the aesthetics I was looking for. I had a time of warmth with myself, while sipping on hot chocolate, and also walked for about 20 mins. I received a call from a good friend in the industry, who told me that I was the first person who came to his mind for a job opening at his firm. That mention itself made me feel very lucky and happy. Again, the power of human connection.

I closed the day, speaking to another ambitious woman and guiding her in her career aspirations. Every time I have these coaching conversations, a part of me feels very happy to meet and speak to such women and a part of me dies, looking at how unutilised their potential is, by the makers of this world and job industry in general. I sipped onto my night detox at that thought and closed for the day.

DAY 32 - 5/9/2024

THE DAY I HAD A PARTICULAR CHAI AGAIN, AFTER HALF A DECADE

The day began on a very bright note—just one of those days when you feel unusually happy and optimistic. My motto this year is to really tune into these feelings and believe in them rather than what others say or what the comparison on social media tells me. At work, I was introduced to authentic Malayali * tea, which I had last tasted on October 11, 2019.

I went on chat + walks with other colleagues, and absolutely relished my conversation with them. I got back to Bettada Hoovu and did a rigorous home workout for the evening. I was scheduled to take a pulmonary function test for my lung capacity today and was initially apprehensive about it. But the doctor turned out to be very supportive. Remembering someone's name is so soothing. I noticed that this doctor remembered every patient's name, as well

---

*   Malayali - Refers to the natives of the South Indian state, Kerala, who speak the language Malayalam

as their ailment and its details. He reaffirmed my faith in this world and that there are still people who care. I returned home after the test and spent the rest of the day just watching some K-drama and making myself some dinner. (32)

DAY 33 - 6/9/2024

THE DAY I HAD PUNDI GASSI AFTER HALF A DECADE

I spent only a little time at Bettada Hoovu, as I had to head elsewhere. I felt it was still significant to document this day because I had one of the most pleasant lunches ever. I had *Pundi Gassi* *, one of my favourite delicacies. As I relished each morsel with gratitude, I felt loved, despite being all alone while eating it. If we all were to bring our attention to the present moment, we would all find something to enjoy and cherish. I took a mini-nap at Bettada Hoovu and then booked my cab to head out. The nap was not a peaceful one - it had its own interruptions by thoughts. But again, I focussed on the comfort of the bed and the soothing sound of the breeze outside, which is a bit louder on the floor where I stay, given it's a penthouse.

---

*   Pundi Gassi - A delicacy of the west coast in the South Indian state of Karnataka, which is a combination of "Pundi" aka rice balls and "Gassi" (ss pronounced as sh of the ship), which is a coconut-based curry made with vegetable or chicken

I appreciate these moments of gratitude that I get blessed with, even on the days I spend only a few hours at Bettada Hoovu.

The Day I Ushered in the First of the Many Amazing Sundays

I came back to Bettada Hoovu only in the evening. I told my mom how living in Bettada Hoovu has improved my Sundays. Having another home that you absolutely love coming back to is a blessing. I am grateful for Bettada Hoovu and how it gives me that comfortable abode.

Sundays are a bit bothersome because they precede an inevitable Monday, which most of us might hate. But would we hate Mondays as much if workplaces/places/people provided us with as much safety as Bettada Hoovu provides me with? I think people hate Mondays in general because of their impending unpredictability. How I wish as a society we all could move towards creating safer spaces so that we may never dread a place or a person.

I cleaned up the rooms and then updated my blackboard for the week when I returned. I figured that the blackboard I purchased is an amazing home decor and adds to my excitement for the week ahead. Having things to look forward to and writing them down is indeed a mood booster. I love the blackboard and the nostalgic feel of wiping it with a wet cloth, the fragrance of the chalk, and the inscription on it. That's all that we did as children here in India. A home decor with a touch of nostalgia and getting back to our roots was a fantastic idea, for which I applaud myself.

DAY 35 - 9/9/2024

THE DAY I SAW 2 FURRY FRIENDS BEING TREATED RIGHT

Let me begin this by stating outright that today was a wonderful day. I had a heartfelt conversation with my colleagues over breakfast, and we exchanged a lot of laughter. I felt the breeze was quite romantic today, and completed about 7k steps in the day.

I went to my workouts with the intent of toning it down for my recovery but ended up lifting much heavier than targeted. There was also a sweet lady who spoke to me at the gym today (it is very rare for people at my gym to speak to one another). Two weeks ago, when I returned to the gym right after having the flu, lifting the same weight left me completely sore; however, I felt perfectly fine today. I appreciate my body for being on the right path to recovery. And of course, the usual highlight of my days, I met Beasty on the way back from the gym. Today I also greeted her humans, and they were indeed very sweet. No wonder 2 of the fabulous good doggos chose them as humans, and Beasty is blessed to have them. On the road next to my flat, I saw a woman feeding a stray dog, and the dog was happily wagging his tail. This was just the most perfect sight ever on an already good evening. Any day when I see kindness towards animals is a good day for me.

I also shopped at the Fab India store near Bettada Hoovu and again felt grateful for the amenities at such a short distance from HSR. The icing on the cake was a top with size S fitting me perfectly, and me musing at myself in the mirror for about 5 minutes. Proud and happy that my investment in my fitness has shown amazing results. What a soul-filling Monday after a long time!

DAY 36 - 10/9/2024

THE DAY I HAD BOTH MY MEALS WITH OTHER GOOD HUMANS

One day, I was barely there at Bettada Hoovu, given a long day at the office, and then meeting my best friend for dinner. But that also explains how fulfilling this day was. I also lunched with a colleague who in turn offered to treat me properly for lunch the next day. I truly felt cherished today.

I ended the day with a coaching call with another ambitious and driven woman, which left me energised and motivated for the next day. Thanks to Bettada Hoovu, I now also write these snippets, which is also something I look forward to every night, something that makes me feel fulfilled at the end of the day. There is something always in our lives that brightens our lives, no matter how stagnant it feels now. We all must find that for ourselves daily.

DAY 37 - 11/9/2024

THE DAY I WATCHED THE SUNRISE WITH MR. KAPEESH

Clear is the theme of the day because I cleared my terrace area of a bit of dust that had accumulated. While I was watching my maid do that, I met up with Mr. Kapeesh, the adult monkey visitor, in the terrace area. He was looking at the rising sun and seemed to be deep in his thoughts. For the first time, I chose to look at him over the rising sun. I also spotted Mr. Kapeesh's extended family chilling on the balcony of the house in the lane behind Bettada Hoovu's house. Coexisting with all creatures around us is indeed beautiful. I went to work, and a kind friend offered to treat me with gluten-free dark chocolate pastry (my choice) and black coffee. I felt special by her gesture, and I also thanked her for it.

I got back home and hit the gym for a dance workout, which was a bit intense today, but as always, it invigorated my soul for the rest of the day. I also noticed a lovely gesture by a stranger today, when she smiled at a stray dog peeing at the tyre of a car in its way. I mused to myself at the purity of that scene. I made myself some vegetables for the day, closed a coaching session with a confident woman, spoke to parents, and ended the day on a fulfilling note.

DAY 38 - 12/9/2024

THE DAY I 1ST ANNOUNCED ABOUT THESE ENTRIES

Today, for the first time, I announced that I would share these stories in the form of a book. I initially felt sceptical, but a kind colleague, who sat next to me, was motivated to still share about it. So, I did. I also took some long walks with colleagues on campus, and this is something I have rarely done since 2020 (COVID times!). The odd climate made me choose yoga for workouts today, and hence I got some time on hand to make some masala makhana for myself.

The best part of the day was sitting on the terrace, reading my book in the company of floating clouds, a mild breeze, and super loud music for the festivities from the neighbouring colony. You might wonder how I read the book or even sat in peace with loud music, but I realised it was the floating clouds and their tapestry that distracted me.

I closed the day with another coaching call with an enthusiastic woman and spoke to my furry family over a video call.

DAY 39 - 13/9/2024

THE DAY I WITNESSED BOTH MISCOMMUNICATION AND PRO-COMMUNICATION

Friday the 13th. Jeez, no scars here, but today was a bit low for me. Without getting into details, I figured it was an instance of gross miscommunication with someone this morning, and I felt quite disappointed at how a minor issue could have been resolved much in advance. The effort needs to be made both ways, though, so eventually I let the situation go because some people never attempt to communicate and solve things. When I got back to Bettada Hoovu, I was still feeling heavy and decided to go for a brisk walk workout today at my usual park. The workout really helped clear my head, and I felt much better after that.

I got back and before I could shower, I spoke to 2 women - Mom and a friend I recently made - to share about this heaviness. I am glad both heard me out and validated how I felt. The beautiful part about this day was that I also spoke openly about a misunderstanding with another close friend of mine and she accepted it with maturity and we had a very open conversation about it.

To every darkness in the world, there is light. To every person who doesn't value you, there is someone who does. I mused on these thoughts to myself. I am glad I still have a very genuine tribe by my side, however small.

I closed the day with a bit of a self-treat, to reward myself for a hectic and packed week.

DAY 40 - 14/9/2024

THE DAY I NAMED CHAMPAK AND PLEDGED MY FRIENDSHIP TO HIM

Please allow me to introduce my newest friend, a black Indie dog on the way to the gym. I first spotted him a few weeks back, trying to befriend all the passersby with anxious and longing eyes. I could tell he was either abandoned or had a troubled experience. I greeted him 1-2 times, and once I also saw him wearing a t-shirt (not sure who tied it up and why), and once sleeping in front of the same house, and once being patted by a passerby. It gave me some hope that maybe he is well taken care of.

But today I figured that while a lot of people do talk to him, he still does not get enough food and is very lonely. I resolved to be his friend and kept thinking of ways to do so during my workout today. I have decided to name him Champak, and the road will now be called Champak Road. So that's in addition to the Victory Road and Beasty road which you would have read about earlier.

The sad part is that while I write about him here and name him, he might be sleeping somewhere all alone and wondering if his existence even makes sense. This is why I always say that no matter how lonely you feel and how hard the night is, there is someone somewhere who is still thinking about you, is influenced by you, and, if you are lucky, misses you.

I tried skincare today, and surprisingly, it turned out super successful. Oh, the joy it gave me! I moved my workouts to the evening, took time to get my bathroom cleaned, and connected with a lady for career coaching. I cooked myself some sauteed mushrooms and green peas, and it turned out better than last time. Overjoyed again! I worked out in the evening (when I met Champak) and then went to the hospital for a minor test that was impending. I decided to push the appointment by 5 minutes to sit there. Why? Convenience.

I closed this fulfilling day by gazing at the crackers being burst for the festivities and the rooftop café nearby, whose lights always make me feel at peace.

The Day I Built a Social Connection with Humans and Their Ancestors

I am physically fatigued but mentally extremely happy, as I write this. I had so many moments to cherish today and so many things to feel good about.

I started my day straight with a leg day at workouts and slayed it. Every time I deadlifted, the trainer exclaimed, "Superb!" It felt like someone was applauding my efforts as I make it daily through this life. I felt extremely high on endorphins today post-workout. I could deadlift without any blisters today, an achievement after many days. Once I got home, I cleaned every corner of the room. As a reward for an already productive day, I cooked myself some Rajma Masala for the first time, which turned out fantastic.

I took a nap and then headed to a book readers' meetup about a km away from Bettada Hoovu. I was glad I chose to show up at this meetup because I met 4 phenomenal and genuine book readers and had a chance to discuss some intriguing topics with them. There were initially just 3 of us, and then we invited 2 girls seated nearby with books in their hands to the meetup. They gladly joined, and all of this just showed how beautiful social connection is.

I got home and thought the day had ended blissfully until I had a surprise encounter with a monkey visitor on Bettada Hoovu. I caught him first trying to open the kitchen window (I actually had a chill in my spine when I saw him doing that!). I tried shooing him away, and he tried attacking me back, making me run inside out of fear. I called up the watchman of the building, and by the time he came by, Mr. Monkey was gone. The watchman then shared some words of suggestion, which I unfortunately couldn't think of earlier. He suggested that I just not interact with Mr. Monkey in any way if he comes back again. Trying to shoo him will be perceived as an attack, and he might attack me back in defence. I felt a bit guilty about trying to scare Mr. Monkey away and decided to be a nice human the next time he visited. As you know by now, I am a promoter of coexistence on this planet (much like the planet Pandora in the movie Avatar).

I ended the day with a mental note of feeling beautiful, inside out, no matter the circumstances, all of this week.

DAY 42 - 16/9/2024

THE DAY I HAD CHAI WITH 4 ADULT MONKEYS

The day began on a rather thrilling note. 4 adult monkeys chose to sit on the terrace area and were chilling to their content. They were seated confidently enough to intimidate both my cook and the grocery delivery guy. The sight of their confidence kept me awake for the next 2 hours, and I decided to put those hours to good use by making myself some chai. The chai turned out very very good, and I relished it while also talking to my parents.

I had been very sore from Sunday's workout and barely even caught any sleep at night, thanks to a very strong pour-over that I had in the evening. I took a call to skip my gym for the day and settle for yoga in the evening. I also gifted myself some foot reflexology and face spa, which I took for the first time. When the body craves attention, one must give it.

I had a rather packed evening as well, with a doctor's appointment (which I had already moved from Saturday), and then marched off to a neighbouring condiment shop to get my favourite set of condiments. I ended up eating one of those condiments for my dinner, which I wasn't happy about. I felt guilty about my choices at the end of the day and had to really remind myself very strongly that I need to be compassionate towards myself as well, as I preach to others to be themselves. I failed to do so today, but I hope I will get better in the coming days.

DAY 43 - 17/9/2024

THE DAY I CHILLED AND WROTE A SEAMLESS LOVE STORY

I tried living up to my promise by pushing my workouts to the evening and extending my sleep by a few hours in the morning. I did not plan anything extravagant and just settled for reading a book and watching a K-drama. I went for a refreshing dance class at 5:30 p.m. and loved every bit of it. I smiled to myself as I walked back and booked the laundry service for the week.

I also noticed that I am now overbooked for the week for my coaching for women offerings. This made me feel truly humble and proud. I am of relevance to someone somewhere and this indeed feels good.

On a side note, I noticed that my writing skills have improved a lot, thanks to these entries that I make regularly. In another document, I was able to write a love story with sheer ease and the required charm, and this has never been easy for me.

Maybe that will also come up as a book someday. Or maybe not, because beautiful things are too precious to be shared.

DAY 44 - 18/9/2024

THE DAY DECORATED WITH COFFEE, TAHINI, CHAMPAK, AND KAPEESH

Mr. Kapeesh(the adult monkey visitor at Bettada Hoovu) attempted to open the kitchen window again today and chilled on the balcony grills for some time.

I set out to explore a new café in the area - Mara Coffee for my morning coffee routine. I visited with my laptop and spent some time there reading a course and sipping on a medium-dark roast cappuccino. Contented with my morning, I got back by afternoon and roasted some sesame seeds for a long pending Tahini attempt.

Before I could attempt it, I woke up from my nap to the sound of Mr. Kapeesh playing with the window again. This time, he seemed persistent about not leaving the balcony grills for some time and was pleasantly munching on some cashews, along with another friend of his. He tried drinking water by turning on the tap in the terrace area and then got scared by the water that came out gushing.

I dared to open the door briefly, and he was seated at the edge of the balcony grill, looking at me with guilty eyes. Now that is something I had least expected. A prankster feeling guilty about their act and showing it so evidently in their eyes. Man. Nature is so precise in how it creates every being on this planet. I closed the tap quickly, smiled at Mr. Kapeesh, and closed the door again. Given the multiple attempts made by Kapeesh to open the kitchen window, I have now decided to place some toy snakes. Of course, this is only to discourage Kapeesh from opening the window (because it looks spooky!) and not harm him in any way.

I got back to attempting *Tahini* *, and realised that it isn't too tasty for an Indian taste bud. Also, it asks for a humongous amount of olive oil, which is beyond the limit of oil I have for the day. Nevertheless, I prepared it with utmost dedication and was happy to finally tick it off my list of to-dos and have a chance to relish it myself.

The best part of the day was meeting my new dog friend, Champak. I intentionally left for my gym a little early to offer him some biscuits. When I first saw Champak, I noticed that he now has a reflective belt meant for dogs to be visible at night and for their safety from vehicles (and drunk drivers). I cannot explain how good this made me feel, that someone on the lane was thoughtful and kind enough to place it on Champak. I walked to the gym and contended that Champak was cared for. I patted him and rushed to the gym.

When I got back from the gym, I made myself some vegetables for dinner and then logged in to a coaching

---

*   Tahini - Middle-eastern condiment made of ground sesame, olive oil and garlic

session with a very determined, resilient, and intelligent woman (who is also a mother to a 7-year-old). I felt deeply humbled and grateful to have been of value to such an amazing woman and to take her a step closer to her ideal job. I closed the day with a short call to my father. My father supported my gesture of not harming Mr. Kapeesh in any way sympathised with his (and other monkeys') situation of struggling to find food in this heavily populated urban area. Coexistence is hereditary, I surmised.

DAY 45 - 19/9/2024

THE DAY I STEPPED OUT FOR BREAKFAST AND GROCERY

Mr. Kapeesh took a break from visiting Bettada Hoovu today. Guess I have successfully deactivated all the prank options for him, but only time will tell. For breakfast, I went to Raghavendra Tiffins today, with an acquaintance I connect a lot with, especially when it comes to fitness. It was ironic that we had mildly loaded carbs for our breakfast and 2 cups of filter coffee, but the time spent was very enriching. What was new today was my visit to a grocery store in person, after I can't even remember when. The experience of searching for what you want, while exploring other options and buying more than you require, and that sheer satisfaction of ticking off all from your grocery list was refreshing after a long time. As you are aware, grocery delivery is now online in India, and in my locality, it arrives in 2-3 minutes. This prevents all of us from stepping out for groceries, even if there is a store barely 100 m away.

I got home to some muscle soreness, which seems to be a common phenomenon since my flu in August. I honoured my body by taking a good nap and opting for a yoga workout today. I also stepped out a bit to look for some good sneakers and failed to find one. It was a bit disappointing, but then I told myself that I now at least know that I must buy sneakers elsewhere or online. Post yoga and dinner, I had a coaching session with a bright young lady, which closed my day on a fulfilling note.

DAY 46 - 20/9/2024

THE DAY I OGLED AT BOTH THE SUN AND THE MOON

Icaptured the big bright sunrise today, too. I am now planning to make this a daily ritual and keep capturing them more often. I decided to take the day slowly, pushing my workout to the evening and reading a book in the morning. I also figured that my average workout recovery is due to a lack of protein in my diet, and I am now planning to make some protein-rich dishes over the weekend. I am excited about it.

I went for my workouts at 5 and spotted my furry friend Champak, blissfully playing with someone. The news about Champak gets better by the day, and I pray and hope it stays the same. Once I got back from the workout, as a promise to myself to eat more protein, I ordered some Rajma and had a good number of vegetables to gain some energy. My mind did play a game by again suggesting I eat less, but I politely shut it down because my recovery from heavy workouts is a priority. I made myself some

Tahini again, given that it turned out extremely tasty on my first attempt.

For tomorrow, I hope to make it to a café known as Heldig, a little away from Bettada Hoovu. I have shortlisted some cafes in Bangalore to explore, and this is one of them. I closed the day, looking at the moon from the terrace area and ogling at the clouds trying to veil its beauty, while I was writing this down.

DAY 47 - 21/9/2024

THE DAY I MADE BASIL GARLIC VEG NOODLES

Picking up from where I left off last night, I made it to Heldig Café! The interiors, ambience, and the coffee were worth it. I got home and did nothing for 30-40 minutes, followed by a coaching session with a wonderful woman who had aspired to be an astronaut once and even had the required degrees. I left the session inspired, and we discussed in the session how women are traditionally told to aim lower than their capability. Energised by an already well-progressing day, I made myself some Basil Garlic Veg Noodles. Well, not sure if that term is valid, but then what I prepared was precisely that. I was very sceptical of how it might turn out and even taste. But I proved myself wrong, pleasantly. The noodles turned out to be sufficient for 2 meals and very delicious. I told myself never to doubt my capability of creating something new because the efforts will add up colourfully (quite literally in this case!).

I took a nap and woke up to heavy showers that lasted just 15 minutes. I was convinced I wouldn't be able to make it for my brisk walk workout today, but then the rains stopped completely, and I had a good workout. Again, never assume that the rains (or bad times) will last perennially; they are bound to end.

I returned home and had the noodles I had prepared in the afternoon. A magical fact about Bettada Hoovu, by the way, is that there are 2 prominent temples and one mosque within a radius of 200 mts, and every day I hear the voice of *azaan* * and the temple bells and prayers very clearly, even from inside the rooms. It is as though the universe is telling me that I got its back. Even today, I dined with Hanuman * and Ganesha * aarti * backdrop sounds, beautifully synced with the azaan. These are the moments that make me realise the beauty of everyday existence and how lovely it would be to document it all my life, as I am doing now.

I closed the day with some K-drama and picked up a new book for my next read.

---

* Azaan - A call for prayer in the mosques

* Hanuman - A deity in Hinduism, known for courage, strength, and utmost devotion to Lord Rama

* Ganesha - A deity in Hinduism known for evading obstacles and the granter of wisdom and knowledge

* Aarti - The worship ceremony of the Hindus, interchangeably used as Pooja as well

DAY 48 - 22/9/2024

The Day I Learnt More About Coexistence with Animals and a Dog Butt Cleaner

I woke up excited and feeling a bit fatigued, thanks to some blaring noise at a nearby school that started right at 5 am (today is a Sunday!). The lack of civic sense sometimes astounds me, especially from a school that is expected to exemplify some of these values. Given that I could not sleep anymore because the speaker volume only got louder and louder, I woke up and made myself some breakfast and coffee.

I was scheduled to go to a nearby pet store + grooming centre, Oh My Dawg, for a session on coexisting with stray animals and being better pet parents. The turnout was less than expected, but I had some good conversations with the speaker and the pet parents who came by. I proudly shared my story of coexisting with the monkey visitor - Kapeesh - at Bettada Hoovu and how easy it is to find a way to co-exist, without harming either of the parties. I kind of expected the turnout would be lesser, but I wanted to stand by the cause I support, which is animal welfare and coexisting with them. I purchased some items for my fur babies and was also amused by a dog butt cleaner, which I might just buy on my next visit. I am glad I went to the store and to the workshop and had a good time at the store.

When I got home, I cooked myself some Moong * curry, which turned out not as great as I had expected. I watched a bit of K-drama and then decided to rest and take a good nap, given that my sleep was mercilessly interrupted in the morning. I woke up late in the evening, feeling a bit better, and took up yoga as my workout for the day.

I closed the day with a call to my mom and picked a fiction thriller that I am very excited to read. It is called Piranesi. Oh, and this is also the start of my birthday week.

---

*   Moong - Translates to Green gram

DAY 49 - 23/9/2024

THE DAY I REDEFINED WHO A HERO IS

The day began very well, given my throat ache had subsided a bit and I had no trace of fever. It was evident that I would be able to make it to the dance class in the evening. Overjoyed, I went on a binge-watching spree of the K-drama, Memories of Alhambra. I have absolutely loved this drama for its very novel concept of an augmented reality game, the authenticity and vulnerability of characters, and of course, top-notch acting by the male lead, Hyun Bin. In the first few episodes, I found myself wondering, "Why is he not getting this problem solved?", "Why is he not able to think such a simple thing?" and so on. I then realised the flaw in that thought. As a male lead and protagonist, this series has let him be flawed and imperfect, which is precisely the series's beauty. Heroes are not those who have solutions to everything. They are those who keep walking despite failing, faltering, and erring, sometimes in the darkness (well, most times). I also rested well before my workouts and completed most of the dance class successfully, with not much coughing.

I got home and then made myself some dosa and ate it with the very expensive gluten-free sauce I purchased for myself. I had a coaching call, then a call with Mom, and then closed the day, reading this book, Piranesi, which is eerily like the way I am journaling these entries. In fact, I was reminded that today's entry was pending when I picked up the book and paused it until I completed it. The book has journal entries in a much more creative way, though. I must admit I felt a bit inferior for not being able to imagine and write so well. But then, that is the whole point of these entries. They are unique to me, unique to this day, and will always remain mine, however imperfect or perfect! (as the reader sees)

DAY 50 - 24/9/2024

THE DAY I NAMED MY ROOMS

It's the day my entries are halfway through! Woohooo! I woke up energised and determined to decide on the names for the 2 rooms at Bettada Hoovu. I am pleased to share that I finalised them, which I will share at the end of this entry.

I went to the gym at 10 am and did a good workout on my shoulders. I am proud of myself for making it to the gym and completing the workout. I got home and cleaned up some garbage, and also ordered some grilled paneer for lunch. It was also my second consecutive day of making picture-perfect and taste-perfect filter coffee. I am also pleased to share that I started a group for discussion of K-dramas and culture and found some 5-6 like-minded people to start the group with. I have always reviewed K-dramas on my Instagram stories and found them a suboptimal expression of how profound, detailed, and emotionally stirring they are. Hence the group, where we will discuss the dramas we are watching, how we felt about them, and more. I am excited to see how this group progresses.

Now, coming to the names I have decided for my rooms:

1. **Shaalemane (The Hall)** - Shaalemane literally translates to "the school house" in my native language, Kannada. In childhood, we would visit our grandmother's house every summer vacation. It is a very fond part of my childhood. There is a primary school in the village, with a seating area, where all the women of the village would gather and chat in the evening. We, the kids, would accompany our mothers/grandmothers and play at the play area in the school, fondly calling it "Shaalemane". I found this name apt for the hall, as this is the place where I work, cook, and create in many ways.

2. **Patnem (The bedroom)** - Patnem is a village in South Goa (again on the western coast of India and a tourism hub). It houses a beach known as Patnem Beach, which I first got introduced to in January 2023. Ever since this beach has been my go-to place for a refreshing break whenever I need it. I have taken many walks and runs on the beach, all of them clearing my mind like never before. Chose this name for my bedroom, as it is indeed a place where I always feel welcome, fresh, and refreshed after I leave it.

A toast to Bettada Hoovu for giving me so many beautiful days ever since I moved here and for these 50 journal entries so far, which I have shared with you, dear reader.

DAY 51 - 6/10/2024

THE DAY I THANKED MY CITY FOR ALL THAT IT OFFERS

I am back to Bettada Hoovu after a break! This is the longest I have been away from Bettada Hoovu, and I found myself doubting what state it would be in. When I reached this afternoon, I found fragments of the white sack in the terrace area (I think I should name this area). I figured they would be byproducts of Mr. Kapeesh's mischief or that of his friends. There was also a Gold flake cigarette packet thrown carelessly, possibly slipped from the hands of the visitor of the terrace above Bettada Hoovu. Nevertheless, I noted the incident and decided to keep a watch on any possible miscreants. I swiftly swept that area and entered to see the rooms completely dustless. Wow!

I thanked Bettada Hoovu for its embrace and started to get ready to head out for an open mic event where I was performing poetry. I picked 4 of my latest poems, which were a bit vulnerable pieces, to test them with the audience. Also, I planned my attire in advance - a black

Puma Tee and black jeans with a Mac lipstick on. The fact that I had thought of my attire in advance made me feel happy because that showed that I was still in the game of this universe and still wanted to show up boldly. As always, I got acquainted with some strangers and found a kind stranger who took my photo and video. This is a norm in all my open mics. My family stays too far away to attend any I have never had a "gang", and whoever I call my friends have never been curious about the things I do passionately (sorry to my friends. You shouldn't know this by my book, I should have told you frankly), which means that I am always at the mercy of the kindness of strangers or the organisers to cheer for me or take my pictures. Guess my talent saves me here. I have managed to make good acquaintances and gathered some fabulous videos and pictures of myself at all the events I have performed.

I got home and left for a brisk walk workout at my usual park. In a pleasant turn of events, I had the entire park to myself for all 30 minutes. I took some pictures to commemorate the phenomenon. While walking, I also felt grateful for the abundance of happiness my city provides. Open mic events, lush and safe parks, clean localities (well, mine is!), and people from all over India to interact with. I also learnt today that Bangalore has about 63 canine protection squads, the highest in India. Often, we complain so much about what we don't have that we don't even make the slightest attempt to know what we have. I mused on this thought and then had my dinner.

I also wanted to share that I have a big day beginning tomorrow. I cannot disclose details as they are personal. But I am glad I have the comfort of Bettada Hoovu to help me ground myself and be ready to take it head-on.

DAY 52 - 8/10/2024

THE DAY I HEARD THE BEST TRACKS OVER A CAB RIDE

This day should be solely dedicated to the sweet incident that happened in the evening. But having said that, the rest of the day was pleasant too. I had a good day at work, though a long one.

Now, coming to the main sweet incident. So, a bit of context - I had a meeting from 5:30 pm to 6 pm on the day, and hence I booked a cab in advance for 6:30 pm. However, my meeting overran quite a lot and I got done only by 7:10 pm. During this time, as already booked, the cab driver started calling me at 6:30 pm once he arrived at the location. Sadly, I couldn't pick up or even message. Given that I work on the busiest road in Bangalore (not an underestimation even if I say busiest in India), I presumed that the driver might call me 3-4 times and look for another customer upon my lack of response. But when I got done with my meeting at 7:10, I noticed that he had called me 15 times.

Out of courtesy, I called him back to apologise, and he offered to drop me back at the same rate since he was still around the location. A bit risky bet (given now this ride won't be tracked by the app), but I chose to take it up. I just had a gut feeling, he would be safe. The ride was not just safe, but a melodious one. The driver started to play all the songs of the 70s by Dr. Rajkumar (a veteran and prominent figure in the Kannada film industry, in India), and ALL of them struck a chord with me. ALL of them moved me to tears, and I felt very grateful for the safe and melodious ride, coupled with the joy of a good day at work and the very famous (but never appreciated) Bangalore climate.

I wondered if these songs would soon fade into nothing, and I wondered if any other customer apart from me would have shut them down cruelly. One never knows tomorrow, but I was glad I was the beneficiary of those songs and the emotions they stirred in me, not anyone else.

DAY 53 - 9/10/2024

THE DAY I EMPATHISED WITH THE BUSIEST OFFICE ROUTE IN INDIA

So, here's an update and a strange insight. I started working at a new job, and it requires me to travel through the nastiest routes in terms of traffic in the whole of India. Ironically, this should be a bother. But I realised that skilfully mastering the time slots you can leave for and from the office, can let you travel the same route when it's much less nasty. All of social media causes upheaval about this route, but no one has attempted to understand why it's so crowded and what can be done to make it better. Say, fewer than 2 % are working on making this better. It's easy to complain about things around us, and sure, they may have traits worth complaining about. But how about being grateful for what it still is and trying to understand it, rather than writing long posts on social media?

I wrapped up my day at work and then hit the gym for a complicated session. I got back home satisfied with my effort and had some high-protein food to cover it up. I spoke to Mom for about 30 minutes and then watched a bit of K-drama before hitting the sack. A weird sense of comfort encompasses my days now. I have resolved to stay with everything I have in my life right now and not badmouth it, though it's unconventional and something general society might disdain. Maybe this is where I have finally achieved a sense of "flow".

DAY 54 - 10/10/2024

The Day I Mastered Staying by My Own Side

I love this date because it reminds me of 1010 signifying new beginnings. Today also happens to be World Mental Health Day. I left for work early and had a packed day. When I returned, I was contemplating going to the gym for a triceps and biceps workout because I had touched upon those muscles yesterday. I decided to still go for it, like 5 minutes prior to the gym time, and I was glad I did. Sometimes, a lot of logic can prevent us from experiencing various other forms of joy, which we may not have even imagined or expected. I hit my personal best in triceps extensions and learnt some new movements too. Both of which I didn't expect would happen. I smiled on the way back home.

Once home, for about 2 hours, I regretted a particular action of mine. This action has been a bit of a pattern for the last 6 years, and I was upset with myself for it. Nobody else told me it was wrong, but I have strongly judged myself for it. Only this time, I decided to sit with it and not escape. I did accompany myself with some good music, but I sat with it. I told myself it was okay to act the same way again because it was something unique to my personality. I may want to refine it, but I shouldn't hate myself for it.

Being human is also about being a bit flawed and understanding that flaws will always exist and don't make us any less (I refrain from saying they make us beautiful or jazz and will leave those words to lyricists in Bollywood movies). Staying by our side is the toughest thing to do, and I am glad I did it today, on World Mental Health Day.

I closed the day with a bit of reading the book, K-drama, and more good music.

DAY 55 - 13/10/2024

THE DAY I PLANNED A PARTY WITH MYSELF

I reached Bettada Hoovu in the evening. It is something I say with pride, that whenever I return to Bettada Hoovu, I restore it back to how it was before I left, within 5-7 minutes, including unpacking whatever I would have carried with me. Some regular activities here include:

1. Stocking up on mandatory groceries for the week

2. Writing the top 4-5 things I am excited about in the week on my blackboard

3. Changing the bedsheets and pillow cover

The latest addition to this list has been preparing masala makhana for the week, which I have gotten much better at now. I found myself musing for a while about who I could celebrate my latest progress in life with, and couldn't think of anyone. This made me feel sad because, apart from my family, I was certain no one would want to share my joy. To elaborate, it's not that there is nobody, whoever 1 or 2 I could think of, are either in another town or are currently attending to some personal exigency. I, however, chose not to wallow in that thought and told myself that this house was a character good enough to join me for any celebrations.

So yes, this Friday or maybe another weekday, I will be planning a party with myself and the house, and the reader is invited to join if you happen to have a time travel machine (jeez, this gave me goosebumps. What if someone truly travels back).

DAY 56 - 14/10/2024

THE DAY SPOKE CANDIDLY AND OPENLY TO 2 AMAZING WOMEN

The day began with an unexpected twist, which happens frequently in Bangalore. Owing to heavy rains last night, the roads were flooded, and I failed to find any cabs or autos to reach the office. I resorted to working from home, despite being very much ready with a new shade of eyeliner and my tiffin box packed. Living in Bangalore is breathing in and out of its unpredictability and dancing with it. However, this gifted me a great cup of filter coffee in the terrace area and some 10 minutes to change my nail colours. I loved how I took care of myself here.

After work, I went to the dance session at the gym, and it was again a downer. The songs, steps, and the trainer weren't to my liking. During the class, I noticed a young lady walking to the trainer and politely talking about the disengaging class. I had an instant admiration for her forthrightness. I left the class after about 60% of it was completed and found her outside as well. I expressed my appreciation for her forthrightness, and we spoke ill of the class for about 5 minutes and exchanged our names. Another aspect I appreciated about her was her confession that she wasn't good at dancing and hence would always prefer a trainer who was clearer on steps, unlike the one we had that day. Once she left, I also spoke to another girl getting ready for the next class. I applaud myself for being candid and open by speaking to both women because I realised I had come a long way in terms of my trust issues with people around me.

I got home from the class and walked for about 20 minutes, in the terrace area (God bless Bettada Hoovu) to compensate for my slightly early exit from the dance class. I also made myself some boiled vegetables for dinner. I packed my breakfast and cucumbers for tomorrow, as I have an early start at the office. This act of self-care made me feel very proud and happy.

The Day I Took Pride in Braving the Literal and the Metaphoric Storms

It rained all night again the previous night. But I had a pre-booked cab which picked me up at 7:45 am, and I reached the office before time. I had a good time at the obviously empty office owing to the heavy rains today. Once I got back, I rested briefly and left for my workouts. It was the deadlift day, and I hit my PR, which is more than my body weight. I can quite literally lift myself now! Haha! Also, I thank the rains for magically pausing only when I had to go for workouts and return to Bettada Hoovu.

After this, the day got draining. It got drained because I was questioned about sharing an opinion about a social issue. I was hurt by how people judged me just for sharing an opinion rather than disagreeing with it and moving on. These were spectators when I was in my troubled times, but they had the time and space to challenge me on my opinions of something that was not even related to them.

I had 2 to 3 silent tears, and that's when I heard the voice of the Azaan from the mosque nearby. This was followed by the regular Tuesday Hanuman aarti at the nearby temple. The only message I took away from both prayers is that maybe, just maybe, someone somewhere is protecting me and I am safe. But having said that, there are 2 things that immensely protected me today:

1. My workplace - I was sipping on coffee and watching the heavy rains lashing outside and people running for shelter. I felt grateful that I had employment and enough income to keep myself warm and enough income to take a pre-booked cab to work. Life is good.

2. Bettada Hoovu (of course!) - For being stocked up with all amenities, uninterrupted power supply, non-judgemental walls that watch me sob, and so much more. I am braving this storm (literally) alone, nestled in the walls of this beautiful house.

I closed my day by penning these thoughts down and having a video call with my cat.

DAY 58 - 16/10/2024

THE DAY I BEFRIENDED COTTON

Any day I see animals being treated kindly is the day that introduces me to miracles. Today was one such day. You might remember my best friend Champak. I saw an old man on the road, inviting him inside and feeding him biscuits. Champak is indeed well taken care of. This is a huge improvement in his situation from the first time I saw him. The second instance where I felt happy was when I successfully made a new friend in my own lane. He is an old furry boy, yet very cheerful. He allowed me to pat him and gleefully accepted some biscuits I always carry in my gym bag. I have decided to name him Cotton (he is fluffy white).

The day was not so pleasant either. I had 2 intruders around 5 pm, and both looked quite scary. I asked them why they were in the terrace area at Bettada Hoovu and they said they were assessing the building for a rental property. This itself made me feel a bit sceptical but fortunately, they didn't have any malice.

I made myself some bread for tomorrow's breakfast and closed the day a bit early, as it was a long one. It's beautiful how in the only time I stepped out today, I witnessed 2 signs of miracle and love. Even while staying indoors, I had someone rooting for my safety. Sometimes, we don't realise we have a lot on our side.

DAY 59 - 17/10/2024

The Day a Mysterious Object Appeared

The day started on a beautiful note. After 3 days of incessant rains and flooding, there was sunshine today. And yes, the sun shone on Bettada Hoovu too, as always. It made me smile. It made me start the day with the belief that no matter how dull and sloppy it gets, the sun always comes, and this is not philosophical. I feel we are all a part of this nature, too, and carry the same traits as the sun, the moon, and the stars.

After a packed day at work, I got home to a not-so-pleasant surprise. I saw a poop, speculated to be either by a human or a monkey or a dog, a little away from the door in the terrace area. Given that the gate to the terrace area was locked, humans and dogs were ruled out. Cats cannot climb as high, leaving only one speculated visitor, Mr. Kapeesh, the monkey visitor to Bettada Hoovu. I was speechless when I saw it and immediately phoned my kind owner to inquire about it. As always, he patiently considered my query and ordered the housekeeping staff to clean it up on priority. The lady from the housekeeping came over with a wide and genuine smile and cleaned it up without a single complaint. She had to come over from a wedding she had been to attend, and I duly apologize for causing her brother. The incident might be unpleasant, but I was rescued, and that's all that matters.

Today also happens to be a full moon day, and the sight of the moon made me feel even better. The racing clouds behind it gave me the illusion of the moon itself moving faster, and everything made me feel so much better. I spent the rest of the day doing yoga, cleaning up some shelves, and then speaking to my parents.

DAY 60 - 18/19/2024

THE DAY I SHOWED UP AND MADE 2 ACQUAINTANCES

Today is a significant day because I made 2 new acquaintances. One was a kind lady at the gym, and another was an uber-friendly dog on the way back from the gym. In both cases, I would credit each of them for caring to see me as another human and interact with me. Yep, it is that simple to make an acquaintance at times. You do not even have to be an extrovert or take a 10-page course on "how to make friends". While I know the name of the human acquaintance, I am yet to name the furry acquaintance.

On the other hand, I was extremely dehydrated and tired in the day, and a leg workout (possibly owing to lack of sleep last night), that too an intense one, was the last thing I wanted to go for. I am not sure what triggered it, but I still decided to go for it. The experience was more rewarding than I imagined. Of course, I got even more battered, but endorphins truly rock. And I made these 2 acquaintances only because I decided to step out for the gym.

Show up, dear friend. And life will be slightly better.

I closed the day with some K-drama, and I was hoping Mr. Kapeesh wouldn't come to the terrace area the next day.

DAY 61 - 19/10/2024

THE DAY I HAD A RAMYUN PARTY WITH MYSELF AND LEARNT MORE ABOUT YAKSHAGANA

The day began on a very unpredictable and morose note.

Reasons - 1) The mysterious poop reappeared on my terrace. My speculations are now not on Mr. Kapeesh, but either a human or a cat.

2) It started raining heavily again after a 2-3 day lull. I had booked a community event for the next day, but that got cancelled due to heavy rain forecasts.

I was already feeling meh for the first half of the day and regretting wasting half of my weekend already. I decided to take some reins of the day and treated myself to some French Press coffee made from beans imported from Rwanda. The coffee came out to be lighter than my liking, but I made a good head start. I took a nap and then decided to record a vlog on mental health and do a bit of office work. I completed both and then went to my usual salon for some self-pampering.

When I stepped out to walk to the salon, I witnessed the beauty the rain had created. The same rain that I was cursing in the morning for ruining my plans had given birth to a very pleasant climate, small plants, and, in general, chirpy people around. I smiled all the way to the salon and took a peek at the lane where I used to stay earlier, to check on the furry friends there. I extended my self-pamper by 30 minutes and then walked to a Korean street food place. The food, ambience, and the provision for solo seats were very welcoming. Having Ramyun, in those rains and that climate, made me feel even more loved by the universe. When I walked back home, I smiled all the way again, having spent the day well.

But the day was far from done. I got a call from a relative+well-wisher+cheerleader of mine from my native village. She inquired about some ideas to generate funds for the revival of a *Yakshagana* * training and performance centre called "Idagunji Mahaganapti Yakshagana Mandali", near my native village. At the end of this day's entry, I have detailed the art form, the need, and its history for anyone else who might be interested in contributing to them in any way, because the sustenance of the art form and the cause is severely endangered.

But speaking for me, when I spoke to this relative of mine, she appreciated the fact that I was planning to

---

* Yakshagana - An ancient folk art and form of worship in coastal Karnataka, a state in South India. This art form is usually performed at night, in an open theatre, and boasts of opulent costumes and head gears along with basic rhythmic musical instruments.

write a book, perform poetry, and also do offbeat things in life, which she said she was very proud of. Such people have constantly reaffirmed and built my confidence in life. People who look at life as something to be lived to the fullest and not treated as a checklist you receive from society, and keep ticking it. I have lived up to the same philosophy, but rarely met people who could see it, and even rarely, appreciate it. I felt grateful that she was one of the extremely few of them.

I called my parents and spoke to them about the cause. They started sharing some stories of them walking 8-10 km in their childhood to watch Yakshagana all through the night and then walking back, exchanging stories with each other and the family. Before the internet, before cell phones, we truly LIVED, and I must tell you, I felt jealous of the purity of their lives.

I closed the beautifully imperfect day after watching a bit of a Bollywood movie.

About Idagunji Mahaganapti Yakshagana Mandali: Founded in 1934 by Keremane Shivarama Hegde, it is a Yakshagana troupe based in the Uttara Kannada district of Karnataka, India. Yakshagana is a folk art mostly performed in the coastal districts of the state of Karnataka, in South India. It was started by Keremane Shivarama Hegde in 1934. He is an exponent of this art form and is the first Yakshagana artist to win the Rashtrapati Award (President's Award), an award handed out by the President of India to people who excel in various fields. The troupe has also been recognised by UNESCO recently. The troupe conducts training, performances, and other affiliated activities for the art of Yakshagana, and is now in urgent need of funds for its revival. Considering Yakshagana is prominent, any company/individual willing to contribute to the cause can reach out to contacts on https://www.yakshaganakeremane.com/

DAY 62 - 20/10/2024

THE DAY I WITNESSED 2 UNEXPECTED MIRACLES

This day, though intentionally slow, affirmed my faith in miracles. For 2 reasons -

1. My sister called me at around 8:30 am to inform me about 9 motherless pups that she had rescued and was planning to safely move them to a nearby rescue centre. The pups were barely 1 month old or less and were dependent on their mother for the milk. However, the mother wasn't seen for the last 3 days and hence was presumed dead (like many stray dogs in India, who roam in search of food for their pups and get killed by cruel humans or their creations). The fact that they were spotted by my sister and were rescued in time was nothing short of a miracle. They have life written in store for them, and I am glad we could play a small part in giving it to them.

2. Around noon, my ex-colleague and a good friend called me to learn more about saving a mother cat

and her 2 kittens. I was pleasantly dumbfounded by that question because this was the second time on the same day that I heard about animals being rescued and cared for. I briefed her about how to care for them and shared some contacts of rescue centres, and I realised that there are indeed kind people in my circle who also share my love for animals. But before everything else, it's a miracle that on the same day, I heard of the successful rescue and protection of animals, which makes me believe that someday, I will have my share of miracles too.

It's a Sunday, and I intentionally did not plan much for the day. I woke up to a slow morning and brewed myself some Durian coffee, which was gifted to me. I realised that the powder was better suited for a cold coffee rather than a hot brew, but I gave it a shot. The brew came out great, and I relished the new taste I was introduced to. I sat for a while in the terrace area and read a book, and then I cooked myself some *Paneer Bhurji** . Bhurji came out way better than expected. I was happy to have made 2 substantial investments in myself in the first half of the day itself, which is cooking something for myself.

This was followed by a quick face mask treatment (K-drama influence!) and watching a Bollywood movie. I also worked out at around 5 pm on my biceps and was very happy with the progress that I had made in strengthening my back and biceps. I returned to Bettada Hoovu, noticed that it was about to rain, and quickly headed out to get myself some healthy snacks. This was more of a reason

---

*   Paneer Bhurji - Mashed cottage cheese

to use my bike, which I hadn't used in the past 3 weeks. Luckily, it cooperated well.

I munched on those snacks and closed the day by changing my nail colours for the upcoming week.

DAY 63 - 22/10/2024

THE DAY I SMILED BACK AT THE SUN

I possibly had one of the best starts to the day this year.

After a mammoth rainfall last night, I was prepared to see devastation around my apartment. Instead, I woke up to a brave, bold sun peeping through the clouds and smiling at me. I smiled back, of course. I instantly made the decision to go for a brisk walk workout at a nearby park, and it was very rewarding. The sunshine was peeping through every little corner of the park, and I could see the municipality workers already on their toes, working hard to clean the city. All of this inspired me to complete my workout with the targeted number of steps and enjoy the workout as well. Once I got home, after a quick shower, I sat in the terrace area and worked for 2-3 hours and sipped on possibly the best filter coffee I made for myself.

The rain started around the afternoon, and I spent the rest of the day indoors. The rains roared outside, and the lightning was the brightest I had ever seen. Nature was truly furious. But the fact that I was watching it from the comfort of the walls of Bettada Hoovu was a comforting one. Despite a challenging day at work, I calmed myself with some book reading and watching one of the K-dramas I had already finished last year. The only time I stepped out was to give some leftover rice to my new friend, Cotton (the white furry friend near my apartment). However, it was a bit of a flop show because he refused to eat it. I spent the rest of the day doing yoga, working a bit, and then speaking some kind words to myself.

DAY 64 - 23/10/2024

THE DAY I MET TOBY AGAIN AND SAW NATURE'S FURY

Today, I was looking forward to a business meeting, and I had planned some time by myself at the Starbucks on campus premises. I was also looking forward to reconnecting with my stray dog friend Toby, who resides at that campus. I befriended him a year ago when I was working at that campus. To my surprise, Toby was still alive and fine and was fast asleep at the same place where I had first met him. What a stroke of miracle! Toby made it through this harsh world (especially to animals) and proved me wrong.

After my business meeting, I was considering going back to the office, but by some gut instinct, I came back to Bettada Hoovu. And I am glad I did so. Around 4 pm that day, the rain gods truly got very wrathful, and it felt like my entire apartment would get submerged. Those were the heaviest rains I had ever witnessed in Bangalore. Once the rain stopped, water had crept in at both Shaalemane and Patnem to a great extent. I spent 45 minutes mopping them dry. I apologised to Bettada Hoovu and thanked him for protecting me from those wrathful rains.

I think this was the day I felt the most grateful about living at Bettada Hoovu and how greatly it protects me.

DAY 65 - 24/10/2024

THE DAY CURIOSITY SHONE BRIGHTLY, AND AS DID THE SUN

After incessant rains for 2 weeks, today was the first day there was not even a drop of rain. But as city dwellers, everyone was too tired from the last 2 weeks to even celebrate this. I made some protein smoothies for myself and reached the office for some meetings. Today, someone at work asked me why I like K-dramas, and I think that is a very commendable gesture. In a world filled with snap judgments, trolls, memes, and hurtful jokes in the façade of a sense of humour, curiosity still shines brightly.

When I got home, I had a bad bout of cold and napped for an hour, taking a half day sick from work. I was almost certain of cancelling my dance workouts in the evening but then decided to at least sit through half of it. The class was so good that I ended up staying through all of it and thoroughly loved it.

Two weeks of unpredictable life left me so drained that I resigned to watching K-drama and doing nothing much for the rest of the day. If you are facing a lot of unpredictability in life, it's ok to be kind to yourself and know that it isn't easy. You may not have people for you, but even if you have a space that provides you comfort and time for yourself, you can still find your own peace. I thank Bettada Hoovu for being that for me.

DAY 66 - 25/10/2024

THE DAY MY SOCIAL ANXIETY WAS FALSIFIED

Today was speculated and rightly concluded to be a very jam-packed day. There was an ethnic day at the office for the pre-Diwali * celebrations, and in the evening, there was a party. I was supposed to head to the office at 2 pm, which meant that the first half of the day I spent at Bettada Hoovu and boy, it was so soothing.

I went to the office for an ethnic day, in ethnic wear, and took wholesome pictures of it. Even at the office party, I enjoyed my time to the fullest, and my anxiety in the morning was completely falsified. I took an auto ride back home and counted my blessings the whole day - a good, comforting and beautiful house, an opportunity to wear ethnic at a vibrant workplace, and an office party where I felt belonged. That's more than what I have had in most of my phases in life. It's still too little compared to what most of my peers have, but it's a lot more than what I have had most times, and for that, I feel abundant.

---

*　Diwali - A prominent festival celebrated in India, also known as the festival of lights

DAY 67 - 26/10/2024

THE DAY I CELEBRATED THE IMPROVEMENTS IN MY LIFE

It is the day I leave Bettada Hoovu for a week to visit my family. I happily turn the calendar to November (yes, I still use the paper table calendar and not on my phone) and make myself a protein smoothie for breakfast. I went for a very good workout session, and on the way back, I even met my best friend, Beasty. Like I always say, the day I meet Beasty is always good, and I immediately drop any expectations for the rest of the day. Today I was also greeted by Beasty's doggo brother - a Rottweiler whose name I don't know yet.

I got home, cleaned the rooms, and made myself a strong cup of filter coffee. Workout, meeting Beasty, cleaning house, *pooja* * for Diwali, and then watched a really sweet K-drama that I am watching currently.

---

*   Pooja - The worship ceremony of the Hindus

I smiled at how my life had improved in a year, though nothing was perfect. The highlight of the day was the realisation of this fact. I locked Bettada Hoovu safely and left for my Diwali time!

DAY 68 - 6/11/2024

THE DAY I HELPED MYSELF BY HELPING SOMEONE ELSE

I was excited about my new glass for my Filter Coffee, and it did complete justice to my anticipation. Thus, I had a blissful morning on the terrace area with my coffee and the relentless eagles flying over Bettada Hoovu. Today was also the birthday of my celeb crush number 2. However, I felt sad that I could not relish his artworks as planned. What a pity it is to get dissolved in the routine of daily life and put your loved one on the back burner.

I geared myself up for a workout at 5 pm, and that further resolved most of my uneasiness. To take some time out for myself, I decided to cancel a coaching session I had at 9 pm. This changed when my coachee messaged me saying she had successfully landed 2 interview calls and attributed it to my guidance - music to my ears. I decided to reschedule the session back to its original time and completed the coaching session, hoping for the best for her.

This whole conversation took me back a bit to the beginning of the year when I was myself in terrible shackles, confusion, and judgements of a job search in the Indian market. It also made me realise how I have beautifully converted that experience to better my coaching skills and even helped many women find the confidence and right jobs. I closed my day with a smile, despite the many folds of heaviness it brought onto me.

DAY 69 - 7/11/2024

THE DAY SOMEONE REMINDED ME TO SMILE

Today was a difficult day, and it lingered on my mind most of the time. Though difficult, when I was lost in my thoughts, an acquaintance just reminded me to smile, which made me feel very happy. We needn't make any grand gestures to make someone feel better; rather, we just need to do the most basic forms of gestures of humanity.

Given the difficult day, I just stuck to my usual routine and did not introduce anything novel. I had a good workout in the evening, which cooled me off enough to rest for the day.

DAY 70 - 8/11/2024

THE DAY I DID YOGA FOR THE FIRST TIME WITH THE SUN

I decided to start the day a bit differently. Hence, I resorted to yoga in the Shalemane area, facing the sun. Oh, and this is a privilege I have because Bettada Hoovu faces towards the east, and hence every sunrise smiles and shines right through the door. I regretted doing this for the first time at Bettada Hoovu, after about 5+ months of living here.

As I had anticipated, this day was long, too. But even amidst the chaos, the cabbies who drove me to and from the office were really kind and professional. This is another thing I am often blessed with, even during my solo travels: the kindness of strangers.

I also realised, for the first time, how super convenient my laundry pickup facility was. I just had to drop a message to them, and boom, in 15 minutes, I saw them at the door for the pickup.

I figured the hack to hack a long day into pieces is sunshine and some kindness.

THE DAY I MADE POPCORN, BOOKMARKS, AND THANKED MY CAT AND BIKE

Today was a productive and fulfilling day, thanks to so many things I could do and enjoy. To start with, I woke up and went for a walk in my favourite park after about 3 weeks. Back to Bettada Hoovu, and I greeted myself with some filter coffee. The view from Bettada Hoovu is something I am proud of every day, but today, it topped the charts in so many ways. So I chose to watch a Hollywood movie with the view as a backdrop, and at 11:11 am, a message popped up in my head which asked me to have a movie date with myself and get some instant popcorn. I ordered one on Blinkit (as I have already shared on many instances, Blinkit delivery takes only 2-3 mins at Bettada Hoovu), and munched on my popcorn in the company of the movie, the wind, and the ever-stunning view from Bettada Hoovu. This was followed by treating myself with some lunch of *Chana masala* * and protein-heavy bread loaves.

However, the key highlight of the day was a bookmark-making workshop that I attended at an art studio and academy nearby. I touched and used crayons after, I think, 15+ years, and made 2 bookmarks for myself. I was also happy with my artwork, which rarely happens when it comes to painting/drawing. The immersion painting/colouring helps us with is something I experienced after possibly more than a decade. I plan to buy a kids' drawing book, and just colour the objects in it, something I used to do when I was a child. The child in us truly needs more of our ear.

After the workshop, I went shopping for an upcoming business trip. I spent more than double the amount I usually spend in a day shopping today, which made me feel truly grateful and abundant. I had begun this year jobless and desperate, and today, I kept no count of the clothes I purchased and happily paid the bill amount. I was right when I told myself that things would change at the close of the year.

All these words and experiences of the day might make you think I would have been happy and chirpy at night. I was sadly anything but that. I spoke to my parents in the hope of feeling better, but that ended up upsetting my mom even more, and she cried profusely. This, in turn, had a chain effect of me feeling worse. The true saviour of this whole scenario and chain of bad moods was my cat, Puff. I tried calling him over the phone, and he responded very happily to my voice and expressed his love to me in his own way - slow blinking, belly rolls, meowing softly,

---

*   Chana Masala - A spicy curry made of chickpeas

looking around for me, and putting his paw inside the teapoy where I play with him. I told myself that until my Puff is breathing on this planet, I promise to live and live well, because his love for me is genuine and pure, for which I am thankful to whoever created this universe (God/science, take your pick).

I also want to thank my two-wheeler vehicle, which I don't treat so well, and yet pushes herself through the merciless roads and the traffic of Bangalore. She is very old, and I am planning to give her up, yet she is here for me.

DAY 72 - 13/11/2024

THE DAY I LIT DIYAS FOR THE 1ST TIME AT BETTADA HOOVU

I am back from Chennai, where I visited for a business trip. The visit was a bit below my plan as I had planned on visiting the beach and my usual place, but couldn't. But there were also some good things like - It didn't rain as much as the forecast had predicted, I had company for all my meals, all my meals were VERY delicious, and last, but not least, I got upgraded to a suite for the first time in my life. I know many of you might have enjoyed that fortune multiple times in life and maybe earlier than me, but for me, this was very special and obviously comforting.

But what is more comforting is Bettada Hoovu. I reached back around 3 pm and was quite drained by the travel. I decided to opt for a yoga workout today and ditch the earlier scheduled leg workout. My workplace had gifted us 2 handmade *diyas* * as part of the corporate gift for Diwali, and I decided to use them today. They are of 2 colours - red and green, and they looked

---

*   Diya - Lamps made of clay or mud

drop-dead gorgeous when I lit them. I kept looking at them for some time, and even as I write this, I am looking at them intermittently. Such is our liking for the light. No wonder we all never want to stay in dark phases and never want to hear the jazz of "it is for the better" and similar token consolation words.

I am about to end this write-up, and they are still alive, and maybe that's why, I will believe in the light that is yet to come in my life. (72)

DAY 73 - 25/11/2024

THE DAY I SMILED A LOT

This day is very significant because, for reasons unknown, I smiled a lot. Every time I smiled, I felt happy for myself. I have been through many phases of life where smiling wasn't easily available or possible. And that is why I felt happy today.

Also, for some reason, I wasn't feeling very energetic. This could possibly be due to a lack of sleep the previous night, but I decided to make it to the dance workout. Magically, my fatigue was repaired completely after the dance workout, and I was glad I made that decision.

I close this write-up by smiling again to feel happy for myself again.

DAY 74 - 28/11/2024

THE DAY I LOCKED EYES WITH CHAMPAK

I left early for work and returned in the evening for some deadlifts. The highlight of my day was meeting Champak, my furry friend on my street. I figured I had not done a great job feeding him the dog food I had procured long ago. The best minute of my day was when I patted Champak, and my eyes met his innocent gaze.

I was physically very fatigued at the end of the day, but I also realised that this tiring yet fulfilling day was what I had dreamt of on most days in my past. Often, we forget that what we have today is what we prayed for in the past. I had a wholesome conversation for 45 minutes with my parents and closed the day with some favourite songs played on the speaker in the Patnem room. Specifically, amongst them was the song "Ishq Bina" from the Bollywood movie Taal, which was released in 1999. I was 9 when I first listened to that song, and while I enjoyed it, I did not grasp the depth of its lyrics. Now that I am 30-something, and have loved and lost and rejected, the song hit the right spot and also made me feel at home.

DAY 75 - 29/11/2024

THE DAY BETTADA HOOVU GOT DISOWNED

A bit of news that let me down today. I learnt from the original owner of Bettada Hoovu that the entire apartment has been sold out to another owner. For a moment, I mused, what felt disappointing? Whether it's the reality that I don't quite "own" Bettada Hoovu or the fact that there will be another change, however minor, in my life.

Either way, I took the next moment to feel grateful to the house owner who has owned the apartment to date and also to the support and cleaning staff at the apartment who do their job flawlessly. As I write this, I realise that I never got a chance to tell them this in person, and I should do so before they change. Only time will tell whether this change is good, bad, or neutral.

This safe haven is also being disturbed by some neighbourhood construction work. It makes me wonder if I even took the silence and serenity of my area for granted all these days. There is so much around us, unnoticed, yet making our lives so much better. Life may not be perfect, but little by little, even inanimate things around us make our existence better.

I close this note by feeling grateful for whatever I have today.

DAY 76 - 2/12/2024

THE DAY I WELCOMED THE LAST MONTH OF THE YEAR, WITH STRENGTH

It's the last month of this year. I find it unbelievable. I began this year at Ultimate Max Pro rock bottom, and as I write this, I can successfully say that I have risen higher. Those quotes on "you are stronger than circumstances, etc," are all true, and I am a living example of it, not because I am some great human, but because we are all remnants of the stars and galaxies, and we can make anything happen.

On that note, I am continuing to stay at Bettada Hoovu. This made me feel very happy, because the thought of leaving this abode, which healed me as much, was quite disappointing, to say the least. At the same time, I have been terribly missing sitting on the terrace area and writing/reading or watching K-drama. It has been either raining or very cold, to sit outside at night.

I hope the sun is out someday this week, and I get to sit and enjoy the sunshine and the view outside soon.

I had a very self-care themed day today, and as I close this write-up, I sit on my chamomile tea and wipe off the clay mask from my face.

DAY 77 - 3/12/2024

THE DAY THAT WAS PACKED WITH MINDFULLY BEAUTIFUL MOMENTS

Today was a very packed day. Some of these packed days often remind me that there is still so much we can get done in a day. And even in its breathlessness, there can still be moments in which we can be present, mindful, and living it up to the maximum.

Let me share some of those moments with you:

1. Someone complimented me, saying I am perfect

2. I laughed very loudly to myself at a joke

3. I spotted my friend Champak, looking for food. Told myself to share some of my food with him - whatever is doggo safe, of course

4. I spotted that black dog at a distance, whom I usually see and smile at

5. I had filter coffee by myself and was in complete peace, in the morning

6. It didn't rain much today, though there was an orange alert issued

7. There was warm sunshine in the morning

8. I brewed some coffee for myself in the evening - this was a coffee powder from Costa Rica

Wow! That's 8 beautiful things on one of the busiest days of the year! Imagine if we were as mindful and present even on the days that are not so busy, how many more beautiful moments we might reap.

Closing the day with a smile on my face, I'm going off to change my nail colour for the week.

The Day I Concluded That I Lived Well

Today is a very happy and beautiful day, and it's ironic I am saying this because once upon a time, this date was the worst day of my life. Today, this day feels like just another day, with its imperfections. Time truly heals, as they say.

I cleaned my bathroom with a regular guy I booked for bathroom cleaning, and he does a fab job, as always. At work, I had some very productive discussions, which added even more to my day. The best parts of the day were the walks I took in my terrace area at Bettada Hoovu in the newly peaking sunshine after 3 days of rain. I just realised that this is ditto, like the exact feelings I have on this day.

I speak to my parents with no specific agenda because I wanted to remind myself that on that dreadful day, I gave them the bad news which reduced them to sheer grief and tears and today I seem to have nothing else to speak about apart from the coconut chutney I am planning to make the next day. I looked at the poster in Patnem (my bedroom in Bettada Hoovu), which had arrived on the same day as that bad day, and I hugged it tightly as I cried like never before. The poster is still there at the same place, unscathed. The poster is of a still from the K-drama The King: Eternal Monarch.

I decided to close the day by watching my all-time favourite Bollywood movie - Dangal. I was wide awake until the date changed to 14th Dec, because I wanted to relish this day's simplicity and its richness too. If you are breathing, hoping, and making food for yourself, believe me, my friend, one-day things will be fine, and you will be fine too. I want you to remember this as you read the entry for this day.

DAY 79 - 14/12/2024

The Day I Availed Foot Reflexology and Some External Validation

The day of sharing all these stories is coming closer, making me feel happy and not anxious. For some reason, I don't have anxiety about whether this will fly or not, because I just want to fly. Today was a day completely free of any plans, and I got some time to dedicate to planning promotion of this beautiful book.

My morning began with a really strong filter coffee I made for myself and then a coconut chutney, which I made for the first time. The chutney turned out to be really good, and I was happy with my cooking skills. I took a quick nap, and once I woke up, some sort of emptiness started to weigh in on me. I told myself that it was totally normal, and decided to stay with it. However, just like a sermon delivered by the sky, I Googled "foot reflexology near me" and discovered a 5-star rated reflexology centre just a km away. I was stumped. I thought that foot reflexology was a distant dream to me, and the only way to avail myself of it was either in Goa in India (where I availed it in July) or in Thailand. We often underestimate what we have with us already and overestimate what is far-reaching for us. The service at this centre was more than worth it, and I was happy with my investment of both time and money.

When I got back to Bettada Hoovu, I cleaned up some garbage at the flat. I also brainstormed some ideas for promoting my book with someone I had only met today. I narrated the idea of this book with my usual apprehension, but it again received the required validation. I told myself to truly throw away my apprehensions along with the garbage I was throwing away and decided to trust this journey with a stronger conviction.

No, I am not against external validations. Let's admit that we are all humans trying to live and survive daily, and not enlightened versions of Lord Buddha, and hence validations truly go a long way, and we all must support each other.

DAY 80 - 15/12/2024

THE DAY I HAD THE ENTIRE PARK TO MYSELF

Today was a particularly bouncy day. I could barely sit for almost the entire day, and the reasons are quite happy. I was either jogging, dancing, cooking, or shopping for my upcoming trip. I particularly enjoyed my lunch and dinner today, both of which were *Ragi Mudde* * and Coconut chutney. Grateful for the taste and the nourishment this food provided me. I spent the morning bathing in the sun and reading my current read, and even for my workouts (which was a jog today), I had the whole park to myself. Yes, that happens if you explore your locality a bit more and have a knack for spotting the right places. I am going on my year-end trip like every year, but this year, I am particularly looking forward to it. For some reason, it feels very abundant and something I am looking forward to.

I had a good nap in the afternoon and grabbed some good coffee before bumping into an acquaintance from the

---

* Ragi Mudde - Finger millet balls, usually eaten with spices or sambhar. A delicacy of Karnataka state, in Southern India

poetry community. Felt good to realise that I had made some genuine acquaintances there. I rushed home and did a bit of quick shopping for my trip, and was satisfied with the packing progress so far. I closed the day by listening to some songs and then just meditating on the day.

DAY 81 - 17/12/2024

THE DAY I FELT HAZY AND GRATEFUL AT THE SAME TIME

A very packed and fulfilling day today. Started with my own reflections on my progress as a professional this year, and I felt glad that I had made substantial progress. I made some racy progress at work and got home on time for the workouts. The workouts got the better of me, and I was quite dazed after it.

I write this after gulping 2 glasses of electrolytes. It doesn't make much difference. Hazy hopes trickle in, and I make peace with just that. These days, I see a black dog in the distance more often and happier, making me smile every single time. In the evening, I heard some crackers outside and missed sitting in the terrace area, which had stopped after the rains and the ongoing sudden drop in the temperature. I feel glad that I relished the best of sitting outside when I could (when there were no rain and the temperature was moderate).

Now that I list these 2, I feel life is still fine. I close another entry with gratitude.

DAY 82 - 25/12/2024

THE DAY I FELT REGRET, VERY DEEPLY

Merry Christmas, everyone! I am just back from my December vacation, and I wanted to pay a visit for 2-3 days at Bettada Hoovu before going to my family for the new year.

I got back here only in the evening, and within 15 minutes, I set the flat back up to what it was before I left for my trip. I was particularly feeling regretful today, about something that happened during the trip. Needless to say, the incident is a bit personal. But today, I realised what regret feels like. It is a feeling where you cannot return to the past but so badly want to go, despite its dangers. You reject the beauty of the present but believe that what happened in the past was more beautiful. I decided to write a poem in dedication to my regret and felt a bit better about it.

But the feeling still lingers. I hope that time will heal it, or maybe a miracle will take me to that moment and reverse it to what I wanted it to be like.

This house shelters me through this regret, telling me that this feeling is safe to feel.

DAY 83 - 26/12/2024

THE DAY I REALISED HOW ART CAN SAVE US

I began the day utterly fatigued by the regret that was eating me up from last night. I made myself a good protein smoothie and then a strong filter coffee. I am particularly looking forward to 2 of the K-dramas that are releasing this week and next week, and also LOVING the current K-drama that I am watching. There is so much art to appreciate. All this did help me overcome the regret I was feeling strongly.

I went to work in the amazingly blissful and beautiful Bangalore weather and returned home later to a gruelling workout at the gym. Life felt abundant. The best parts of the day were my 2 furry best friends, Beasty and Champak, being pampered by some strangers around them. It felt good to see my tribe not too far from me.

I also got onto drafting my goals for 2025 - a ritual I do every year in the last week of December. While doing this, I also need to refer to the past year's goals, and when I looked at my goals from last year, I was proud of myself.

This was not for having achieved/not achieved those goals, but for the clarity I have this year about my goals. Sometimes, our success is not in achieving the goals, but in having built the ability to have finer goals. On that happy note, I close today's note with some Bollywood music in the background.

THE DAY I WALKED TO HAVE CHAI AND REALISED I INSPIRE

The day began on a very good note, with the terrace space being cleaned after many days. It feels like a mental block that got cleared. I took a nap after that and woke up at 9 am to log in for work. I also soaked myself in some sunshine that came up in the morning. After a great day at work, I headed out to my gym, which I initially planned not to. I performed better than I expected myself to at the gym. I got home and craved some chai at a place just 500 m from Bettada Hoovu. I thought I could just order and drink, but something made me just take that walk and have chai. And, I was glad I did that.

I returned and had my dinner, and then spoke to an ex-colleague. During our conversation, she mentioned that she finds it inspiring how I live my life, which is on my own terms and very authentically. This is a huge compliment because, on my low days, I feel regretful about some of the choices I have made in my life. We all live a harsh reality, in our own way, and the least we can do is say something we appreciate in another person. I am grateful that I experienced that today.

I closed the day with some chamomile tea and electronic music.

DAY 85 - 28/12/2024

The Day I Got Befriended by a Sweet Cow and Bought Lavender Home Decor

I loved today for so many reasons. I began the day by marching off to a nearby Masal dose * (the pronunciation in the local language and my native tongue for Masala dosa) place and relished it for my breakfast.

At the restaurant, a very gentle cow came up to me on her own and demanded pats. This felt like a huge compliment to me, that she chose to come to me in the crowd there. I took her well wishes and headed out to what was the most daunting challenge of the day - visiting the dentist. They say you haven't properly lived alone unless you have been to the dentist all by yourself. I met that goal today, haha! I was quite anxious and nervous as

---

*   Masal Dose - A South Indian dish made of fermented batter of boiled rice and various legumes. The fermented batter is used to make pancakes and stuffed with a potato-based filling, which is eaten with Sambar/Chutney/Any spicy curry

expected before any dentist visit, and waited for my turn. The diagnosis of my issue turned out to be something normal, and I was recommended 2 tooth fillings with minimal invasion. I would also like to acknowledge and applaud the team of doctors who helped me during the consultation. Point to note here: This top-notch clinic was hardly 50 steps away from Bettada Hoovu, and for the umpteenth time, I felt grateful to be living in this area.

I got home and made myself some Sambar for the first time. The *sambar* * turned out a bit below par, and I decided to redo it at night. I took a very good nap in the afternoon and decided to resort to yoga to restore some flexibility back into my body post my trip. I also ordered some storage containers for my wardrobe, and it felt beyond peaceful to look at the clutter in my wardrobe now placed in lavender containers made of jute. I closed the day with a big bang conclusion about the travel destination I will be off to next year. Cannot disclose it now, but soon after I concluded that, very happy music started playing on the phone, and I took it as a signal from the universe.

---

*   Sambar - A spicy lentil curry made in South India, usually eaten with rice, optionally with mixed vegetables added to it

DAY 86 - 5/1/2025

THE DAY REARRANGED AND CLEARED AND COOKED AND CHERISHED THE NEW YEAR

I just realised this is my first entry of this year! Happy New Year to all!

I got back to Bettada Hoovu around the evening, and had a great time, because of the following:

1. Cooked masala makhana after a long time

2. Threw away stuff that I hadn't used for a long

3. Changed my nail colour

4. Added 3 new home decor items to Bettada Hoovu - 2 posters and 1 lantern

The most satisfying of all was clearing up the stuff that was no longer useful. Just felt like throwing away those beliefs that were of no use to me anymore. Out of the 2 posters that I ordered for my home decor, I would like to share one of those, which I particularly like. "Actually, life is beautiful and I have time." What a lovely thought to live by. It is never too late to throw away something that is of no use to you anymore. Life is possibly better on the other side of it.

Loving the start of this year. Loving the first day of the year at Bettada Hoovu!

I closed the day with some chamomile tea and a newly released K-drama, which I am enjoying a lot.

DAY 87 - 6/1/2025

THE DAY I TOOK A WRONG TURN, BUT REACHED JUST FINE

It's getting colder in Bangalore now, and I woke up to a cold morning. In temperature, yes, but also because this was the first one after the December vacation and New Year's. I have been dreading this day for the last 2-3 days, and now it is here. I booked a cab in advance for my pickup and also for my return, just to eliminate the unpredictability of finding a cab on this already bothersome day.

My cab arrived on time, and the driver seemed professional—until he ignorantly missed a turn, which added 30 minutes to the already insanely long drive owing to peak-time traffic. Bangaloreans can empathise with how hellish this can feel. And yes, I felt the same. I reached the office later than planned, but thankfully, I had a good day.

Once back to Bettada Hoovu, I picked myself up for a dance workout. The day was long, but I am glad I still picked myself up for the class and did my best. Now that

I write this, I realise that despite a bad start to the day, it still ended on a note that I can smile about. And maybe that's why we should entrust our faith in the days/years/ journeys that sometimes start on the wrong note. Nothing was damaged with one chance of benefit of the doubt.

I closed the day with chamomile tea and watched viral cat videos on my phone.

DAY 88 - 7/1/2025

THE DAY I DISCOVERED THE CHIRPY BUSH AND A KIND DENTIST

As I write this, I am wondering if I am writing after 2 days or 1 day. I realised it was just 1 day! I began the day on a good note by deciding to WFH, which brought me 30 minutes extra sleep. When I woke up, I made myself a perfect filter coffee and noticed something very beautiful near Bettada Hoovu for the first time.

It was a lush green tree filled with birds chirping happily. I wondered why I hadn't noticed them earlier. I also wondered how beautiful Bettada Hoovu's surroundings were. Despite living here for more than half a year, there were still so many things I hadn't noticed, and they were all so beautiful. I took a video of their chirps and then headed indoors for some work.

I had a good gym workout in the evening and then had to visit the dentist for a follow-up. What I thought was a regular check turned out to be a re-cleaning and polishing session for my teeth, and I was a bit taken aback. Nevertheless, the experience was umpteen times better thanks to an uber-sweet dentist who calmed me down. Surprises, harsh truths, bitter life, like everything, can feel better with kind people around, I mused. I walked back and found all the medicines just 100 m from Bettada Hoovu, and then dined while working in parallel.

The highlight of the day was 1 person on this planet checking with me how my day was, for which I feel very grateful.

DAY 89 - 15/1/2025

THE DAY I SAW THE SUN TAKING A SELFIE IN MY MIRROR

I began the day by ogling at a very bright sunrise. I also caught a shot of the sun peeping into the mirror near the entrance of Bettada Hoovu today. This was also something I noticed for the 1st time at Bettada Hoovu.

I made myself a perfect filter coffee (again!) and then logged into a busy day at work. I worked on my triceps today at the gym and while on the way back, I spotted my best friend, Beasty. She happily wagged her tail, though she was inside the gate and I felt happy that I had at least one person (furry person) near Bettada Hoovu who was happy to see me. I got home and ate a very tasty dinner, which my cook had prepared.

Today, however, was a significant day, because I announced and introduced this book for the very first time on social media. The response was way better than expected. I always felt that my achievements and goals were too unconventional for our society, and I would struggle to find cheerleaders or supporters. While that is still partially true, I am glad I was partially proven wrong today. Gratitude for whoever still believes in me and my dreams!

DAY 90 - 16/1/2025

THE DAY I LOST TO FATE, AGAIN

Ido not know how and where to start today's entry. My eyes are too blurry and weak, thanks to the tears I have shed all day. My hands move on autopilot, as though rage fills them. Rage, for not being able to save what I loved the most. While they are on autopilot, they also shiver. Possibly begging some Almighty if he/she even exists. I cannot name what I feel. I don't know if it's rage, fear, helplessness, or wanting to control; I truly don't know. I am devastated. I failed to save my most prized possession, my Bettada Hoovu.

With profound sadness, I share that I was asked to vacate Bettada Hoovu today. The message arrived via our building caretaker, quite apathetically delivered both by him and the new owner of Bettada Hoovu. Upon speaking to the owner, I could get an extension of 1 month of stay, but not beyond. I broke down the moment it was told to me, and had it not been for the 2 colleagues seated next to me, I would have plummeted into a deeper abyss. This place gave me hope, a reason to look forward to, a reason to believe in life, a reason to believe in good times, amongst a host of many other things. All day, all incidents of the past kept trickling down to me, where I couldn't save people and animals I had loved, and keep them forever with me. I am a mess today.

Do we ever own anything? People, material possessions, and even our own lives. Nothing is ours. Everything is rented to us, just like Bettada Hoovu was to me. We all live and thrive on borrowed items and hope to make the best of them until we can. I did not and never intended to end my entries this way, but here it is. There is no escape, only surrender to fate.

On this dreadfully long day, I want to share something someone at the office shared with me. When I said that all good things had happened to me because of Bettada Hoovu and now they might cease once I leave, she told me that good things happened because I deserved them, not because of Bettada Hoovu. And maybe just because of that, I only mildly believe that I will be able to make a home in another house that I move into. Maybe I am the soul this house had, which made it home. And I get to carry that soul with me, somewhere else.

I hope this feeling has some end to it, like my stay at Bettada Hoovu - a home I built with the best of my love, effort, prayers, and many emotions, which now I have to let go. But I don't know how. Seems like only money could have saved my Bettada Hoovu, but I have everything else apart from that. Love, honesty, commitment, loyalty, affection. Guess none of it matters, just like it doesn't anywhere else in the world either.

I crashed asleep (or maybe unconscious) when my eyes and head couldn't hold the tears anymore.

DAY 91 - 18/1/2025

THE DAY THE UNIVERSE GIFTED ME 107 MICROSECONDS OF GRATITUDE

Most of the day, I feel like either sleeping or working and not giving any breathing space to my thoughts. The moment a breathing space comes in, I end up in tears. Rage fills me often and takes the best of my breath and mindspace. By some God's grace, this is a weekend and I can afford to be at my worst.

I woke up and dragged myself out to the gym, hoping for endorphins to make me feel better. It worked. I even smiled and spoke to another girl at the gym, and if you have read my entries, this is better than most of my days at the gym. On the way back, rather than playing with Champak or Beasty, I am looking at the gates of various houses on the way for any open vacancy for a flat. Tears kept filling my eyes. I see people joyous, coupled, and laughing their hearts out in these houses, but no vacancies for flats. It filled me with rage again. Why can't joy ever be mine? Why can't all the things I love stay with me forever?

Even in this mindlessness, I discovered another beautiful road in my locality, and it filled me with gratitude for a microsecond - an improvement over the last 2 days.

I made myself some Paneer Bhurji, listening to some peaceful tracks a kind friend sent me. They are indeed peaceful, and I relished my Paneer Bhurji. I took a nap and again woke up with tears to head out for the flat search. I felt another microsecond of gratitude because of the resources I can afford even in this despair. I eventually bumped into a very similar penthouse property not too far away from Bettada Hoovu, and it filled me with 5 microseconds of gratitude. This bolstered my hope immensely, and I could feel that the universe was still watching over me.

What happened next was even more surprising. I received pictures of the same rental property from another broker, which intrigued me. Some call of the universe made me call him and actually ask for more such penthouse suggestions. This led to finalising my next flat. Another penthouse. A km away from Bettada Hoovu. I felt relief and gratitude both for 100 microseconds. I spent the rest of the night thinking about Beasty, my walks back from the gym, many phases and thoughts during that walk, the feeling of pride during those walks, the peace this locality offered me when the rest of my life was messier than an airplane crash, the regret of never having been to a fruit mart near Bettada Hoovu, and so much more. The collage of memories and emotions associated with them made me feel bad about feeling everything so deeply. But then, I got to accept myself and love myself the way I am.

For the past 2 days, I have even wondered if I had gone mad, clinging to such material possessions. The last time I was as devastated was when my grandfather and a close friend passed away unexpectedly. Maybe it doesn't need to make sense. It doesn't need to be compared. I honour every emotion and effort I have put into Bettada Hoovu.

"Sometimes I wish I wouldn't care, but then I wouldn't be me."

DAY 92 - 19/1/2025

THE DAY AN EAGLE DELIVERED ME A MESSAGE

I felt better today. Occasional teardrops but not a lot of them. Someone asked me today, "Are you happy now? Now that you've found another flat?" I said, "Relieved, yes, not happy. I will never be happy to leave my Bettada Hoovu."

I woke up to the temple bells this morning, again making me realise I would miss them. The day began with unseasonal rains which shocked everyone in the city, and it felt like maybe it was in nature to keep shocking us. I took it slow in the morning and had my coffee outside in the rain because another guilt I have is not being able to spend enough days in the terrace area at night. Rain and cold weather kept interrupting. I decided to order some food for lunch, to be able to spend more time with my emotions.

After my bath, when I went out on the balcony to dry my hair, I noticed the dark clouds travelling slowly away from the city. I pictured them as my current fate, but what slapped me back to my senses was the sight of an eagle sitting firmly on a water tank right behind Bettada Hoovu. He was unbudged, in his own world, despite the clouds hovering over his head. Maybe this eagle was the spirit animal the universe wanted me to adopt, I told myself.

After my gym in the evening, I intentionally choose a longer route back home to enjoy the lush green canopy all through my locality. Though I am just going about 1 km away, I won't be living here in a few days, and these gorgeous green canopies were one of my most favourite things near Bettada Hoovu. I still tried looking for any vacant flats around Bettada Hoovu, with a dying hope of finding something around (yes, I have booked another flat, but my heart refuses to accept).

I spent the rest of the evening just watching some movies and relishing Veg Thupka, from a nearby restaurant (it won't be nearby anymore! Tears!).

DAY 93 - 20/1/2025

THE DAY I BEFRIENDED A TRI-COLOURED PUPPY

The day began with informing my regular maid/cook about my change of house. Luckily, she agreed with my opinion that this move was very unfair to me. I went to the office a bit mindlessly, but thankfully, some really kind colleagues made my day. A laugh exchanged with someone can go a long way. The workday went quickly, and I got back home for a deadlift workout. I took the longer route again to Bettada Hoovu. Again, I looked for any new flat vacancies, to no avail.

What I did see was a tiny puppy with 3 shades of colours on him(brown, black, and white) loitering around in search of water. I called him and tried patting him. He happily licked my feet, and I felt guilty for not carrying any dog food. He seemed very weak, and looking at him scavenging for food, I thought he would follow me. To my surprise, he got distracted by a pink slipper, discarded by someone, and started playing with it. I smiled and thanked him for teaching me how to play even when distressed. Not that I have still mastered it.

I got back to Bettada Hoovu and finished my laundry. After dinner, I tried sitting outside in the terrace area to relish whatever I could before leaving, however cold it was. Unfortunately, it was cold enough to make me go inside within 10 minutes. I got in, finished a coaching session with an ambitious woman, and then got to my K-dramas.

Coaching women lifted me even last year, this time. And I felt grateful that it came to my rescue even today.

DAY 94 - 22/1/2025

THE DAY BOLLYWOOD MUSIC SAVED ME

I woke up feeling very tired, thanks to a long day the previous day. I took a quick nap, and since it was a WFH day, I felt a little grateful about the day. Ever since I learnt that I would be leaving Bettada Hoovu, I have been trying to glimpse the black dog in the distance, who often brings a smile to my face. I failed to spot him the past few days, but thankfully, today I spotted him at his usual spot (which is in the distance hence his name). I smiled today, too, when I saw him (I just realised I didn't know if it was him/her since I always see him from a km away). I instantly took a picture of him and of the sunrays, as I have been doing since last week.

I spent the day relishing my filter coffee and savouring all the uncontrollable emotions that kept pouring on me like the incessant rains at my native on the west coast of India. I did not stop them. Not even a bit. My house deserves as much. What kept me company in this was nature. My solo plant, whom I have named Purple, was basking in the sunshine. An eagle soared higher and higher, and birds chirped happily. All of them tried their best to make me feel better. I kept gazing at the trees near Bettada Hoovu longingly until they imprinted in my mind.

My workout today was a dance workout, which I enjoyed a lot. I started off quite weak, with no intent to enjoy the dance, but just to do it to get whatever minimal endorphins. Surprisingly, at the end of the class, I felt even more energised and truly enjoyed the dance, which I was failing at the beginning. Maybe my grief will get better, too, I thought to myself. I got back to Bettada Hoovu (by taking the long route again) and blasted my head off with some Bollywood music. I have never liked them much, but one particular song helped me feel better today.

I don't know how and when I will heal, but I at least showed up to life today, I told myself.

DAY 95 - 23/1/2025

THE DAY I SHED A TEAR ON THE VICTORY ROAD

Last night, before sleeping, my mom sent me a text saying, "I hope all your pain disappears in the morning". Seems like some God heard it, and I felt way better this morning. I woke up to a slow morning, clicked the picture of the sunrise, and then had my breakfast and coffee in joy.

I even closed my work before the anticipated time and headed to the gym for an overhead squat workout. On my way back, I said hi to Beasty, and she wagged her tail as usual. My heart did not let me stay longer, because I still feel very sad about not being able to see her every day. I still walk with a slouch and a weird inferiority complex about being unable to keep what I love for myself. I still keep looking at buildings for any vacant flats. Today, while walking on the victory road, I remembered how I first named it and mentioned it in my entries. A drop of tear rolled off, but nothing more. I also looked at my

2 furry friends, Ferrero and Rocher, and silently apologised to them.

I then headed for a long-awaited foot reflexology session to get rid of the pent-up stress in my feet. I felt grateful that this reflexology place was still accessible to me from my new flat. I got back home, had my dinner, and then video-called my furry family back home, especially my cat, Puff, whom I hadn't spoken to for a week. Life is stabilising. Sun rays are peeping in, and I am trying to flow with the river.

DAY 96 - 24/1/2025

THE DAY I SMILED AT THE SUN RAYS FROM THE SUNSET

I have been taking late cabs to work, to spend my time having my filter coffee with Bettada Hoovu. It has soothed me to a great extent. When I got back from the office today, I had a quick nap and swapped my daily workouts for a yoga session. I noticed another beautiful thing today: the sun rays from the west, during the sunset, falling beautifully on the tapestry in my bedroom. The sight lulled me to a blissful sleep, and I wondered if we start noticing the beauty in people and places strongly when we were about to lose them.

I stepped out for a flu shot, which was due this month. I visited a new tea shop and tasted my chai with ease, smiling to myself over the sight of happy people around me. On my way back, I took bike rides in my locality around Bettada Hoovu. While this was to keep rounding the area, it was also to look for my friend Champak, whom I hadn't seen for 3 days. I couldn't find him today either.

When I got back from my ride, I listened to music and did nothing gigantic. The flu shot also numbed me, and I remembered the time I was struck by the serious flu in August when this house had cared for and protected me when no human came to help.

THE DAY I GOT REMINDED OF MY PREVIOUS BETTADA HOOVU

I began the day by shooting time-lapse reels of mine, making a French Press for myself. Yes, this could have been done countless times earlier, but now I am pressed for time. We always assume we have a lot of time, not realising we all live in rented time, just like our houses. My reels became a hit and garnered the most views any of my videos/reels have ever had. When I looked at the reel and saw the trees swaying in the backdrop, my heart sank a bit. I sat out in the terrace area and had the company of eagles, their whistles, and the happily chirping birds in the tree next to Bettada Hoovu. I smiled at both of them.

I made some chole for myself and decided to work out at Bettada Hoovu itself, cancelling all gym bookings for the day. I had a good nap and woke up to the rental agreement of the new place I booked last week. It triggered the formality of the end of my stay here, and tears came out gushing. I cried till I couldn't make sense of time, and I let it go that way. When I felt it was beyond my control,

I called up a friend and then my family. I am grateful that I called each of them because when I called my family, my sister reminded me of a blog I wrote while leaving my previous flat, where I had lived for 2.5 years. The last line of that blog read, "I am confident of making any place home, anywhere". It's funny, it pacified me instantly. My own words encouraged me to look ahead and have confidence in myself. At least for the night, I could compose myself and then fall asleep.

DAY 98 - 26/1/2025

THE DAY OF LONG WALKS AND LONG RIDES

I began the day with a very good brisk walk workout at my favourite park nearby. At the end of the walk, I took a very long walk in the entire area, again looking for any flat vacancies. While I have lived here for 3 years, every time I take a walk in the locality, I am mind-blown by its beauty and serenity. I took some pictures during the walk and got back to Bettada Hoovu in tears (again).

However, I want to share that today I discovered a way to put an end to this unfortunate chapter and tears in a very constructive way, and I will share about it soon enough. I headed out for an open mic poetry event at one of the most commercial hubs in Bangalore - Indiranagar. After my event, I discovered and witnessed a heartwarming story that happened live, at the bookstore where my performance was. A dog that had escaped its caretaker had roamed to the bookstore, and the kind owner of the store took care of her and even accompanied her as she sniffed her way back to her caretaker. Apparently, the dog was abandoned by her previous owners once they shifted abroad, and this caretaker had been feeding her ever since. The story made me feel happy and believe more in the goodwill this universe has.

On my way back, I observed the vibrant streets of Indiranagar, filled with people who wanted to drink, make merry, and make the best of the remaining weekend (this day was a Sunday). I appreciate the glitter, and everyone has their way of spending the weekend. But noticing Indiranagar in its glory made me feel even more grateful towards my own locality and the serenity it offers, despite being in a bustling metro city like Bangalore. I smiled at the thought and spent the rest of my ride back to Bettada Hoovu reflecting on the day.

DAY 99 - 27/1/2025

The Day I Saw the Black Dog Along with His/Her Human

Today began on a beautiful note. I woke up and stepped outside to capture the sight of the black dog in the distance (the usual fellow who inspires me and makes me smile) and a human playing with him. Felt like I was given a chance to peek into the parallel universe. I made a mental note to meet that black dog in the distance one day.

I then made a coffee for myself and breakfast and shot an absolutely breathtaking picture of the sun. The sun was a bit too strong, so I turned around and faced the door of Bettada Hoovu, and we had a good coffee date. I also noticed that the eagles that keep soaring in the sky regularly photobomb any shot I try to take of the sky.

I got in and figured some time out to make masala makhana for myself and then get ready for a minor blood test. I also did pooja today after many days, because I was angry with the Almighty ever since I got to know that I had to leave Bettada Hoovu. I went to the gym and had a good time, and on my long walk back, I kept ogling at the houses in the area. I particularly looked at the penthouses in each of these buildings and felt jealous. How rich must those people be to be able to live in such a beautiful area and safeguard their stay there, which I clearly failed to do. I walked on the lane where Cotton and Jimmi sat and smiled when I saw them sitting blissfully.

At night, after dinner, I shot some pictures of myself working from the terrace area as a memory and marvelled at the fighter jets that flew in the sky. They were mesmerised by the bats and their screeches, from a tree about 100 m away. I gave a long sigh before moving inside, as the winds were getting colder. I am happy I cried much less today, and a new idea of a romantic story came to me, just like those fireworks that sometimes light up the sky near Bettada Hoovu.

DAY 100 - 29/1/2025

THE DAY I DECIDED TO KEEP WALKING

Today is the 100th entry I share with you. How I had visualised my 100th day to be was completely different. I expected myself to be overjoyed, full of smiles, cosy, and chilling at Bettada Hoovu. On the contrary, I am just fine today. Looking for tiny hopes from the universe, trying to stay in the terrace area only to run inside due to cold winds, trying to relish my walk on the Victory Road and Beasty Road, not knowing when it would be the last, and so on.

Champak is still missing on the road, and now I haven't seen him for 10+ days. Something I never expected I would record in my 100th entry. Unusual things have inspired me these days. The top 2 of them are Bangalore traffic and Bollywood songs. I am surprised as I write this, but it's true.

I had my morning coffee sitting straight facing the sun. I said hi to Beasty, who now sits inside her house, but wags her tail as always when she sees me. I saw Cotton being cared for by a family in the neighbouring building, and these few things made me smile. I had earlier planned on ending my entries in this book at 100, but I decided to continue only because of the shattering news of having to leave this place and wanting to record more of my days here. And that is possibly the only good thing about it.

I have decided to keep documenting my days at Bettada Hoovu until I leave, and maybe also host a farewell party for it. Thoughts keep trickling randomly, I am just trying to live by the day and spend as much time as possible at Bettada Hoovu.

DAY 101 - 2/2/2025

THE DAY I MADE A LIST OF DIFFERENT TYPES OF GOODBYES

On the day I got to know I needed to leave Bettada Hoovu (16/1/2025, I will never forget the date), a few of my colleagues shared some gem-worthy words. I can now absorb them well, and I also want to share them with you:

1. Good things happened to you because you deserved them, not because of the house

2. You will make another house your home, too

3. You faced tougher things; you will face this one, too

4. Maybe your good phase has started, and that's why it will continue to be good

5. Not everyone will understand what you are going through, and that is ok

6. You should plan a farewell for your flat

I have taken the last one, in particular, seriously, and have made a list of farewell parties for Bettada Hoovu. I did give a thought to calling in people, but 98% of it would only be me and Purple, the tiny plant I have been growing since July 2024 (also when I started writing these entries). Of course, I cannot miss out on counting the biggest and the best companion. The house itself.

The climate has suddenly gotten hotter, making it possible to sit on the terrace as though it heard my plea. I also noticed a fighter plane flying above the terrace area at night, and it was a beautiful sight.

DAY 102 - 3/2/2025

THE DAY I PLAYED WITH JIMMI

Quite surprisingly, even the universe is trying to give me closure on multiple levels. Today, when I was returning from the gym, I met Jimmi, with whose friendship I started these entries. I played with him for 15 minutes, and I could see so much affection and gratitude in his eyes. He is an old boy, and I feel so lucky to have met him.

I returned to the apartment to notice that the lift had stopped working, and moreover, our very diligent caretakers had been released from their services. Now I had no one to reach out to for any help, and our apartment also became vulnerable to theft/trespassing. I hate to say this, but for the 1st time, I saw some merit in leaving Bettada Hoovu. A soft voice echoed in my heart, "What have people done to this beautiful abode?"

DAY 103 - 4/2/2025

THE DAY I GOT THE MOST IMPORTANT CLOSURE

Today is the day, it has become even more confirmed that I can leave this place peacefully. I saw Champak, after 3+ weeks, hale and healthy and running around like he usually does. And there is no greater happiness or closure than this. As I write this, the eagle whistles loudly and sweeps across Bettada Hoovu, nearly colliding with the penthouse cover. Guess that was him/her trying to cheer me up.

DAY 104 - 5/2/2025

THE DAY OF THE MOVIE NIGHT FAREWELL

As though the previous instances of closure weren't enough, today, the tapestry in the Patnem room broke off on its own and fell. I was tempted to stick it back, but I took that as another sign of closure, folded it, and kept it inside the cupboard. Today, I had also planned the lst phase of farewell - a movie night on the terrace. I chose the movie "The Wild Robot" and made some masala makhana for myself for the company. I considered placing my roommate and plant, Purple, on the table, but I figured it had a muddy base and returned it to its original place on the basin.

DAY 105 - 10/2/2025

THE DAY I LEARNT WHAT HAPPENS TO LOVELY THINGS

I have started to observe the leaves around me falling a bit more, listen to the whistles of the eagle a bit more, and close my eyes whenever the temple bells ring and the azaan is made. Every moment here feels like a bonus. The falling leaves tell me that if the tree can let go of its own leaf when it's time, then who am I to refuse to let go of this house?

The date of my shift has now been finalised, and it is a bit later than planned, which brings me great joy. Last evening, I watched Champak roam around happily and freely, and that made me smile very widely. I am slowly coming to terms with the truth of all of this happening, both fortunate and unfortunate.

I read something on Instagram today that felt very relevant and insightful: "Lovely things come and go, but at least they come." And yes, to every lovely thing or person that has happened to me (like Bettada Hoovu) but is no longer with me, what a stroke of luck it was to have spent time with you, in a world where so many dreadful things exist and can happen.

DAY 106 - 12/2/2025

THE DAY COTTON PLAYED WITH ME

This is the most annoying week of the whole year, whether single or coupled - Valentine's week. I know, unpopular opinion. But sometimes, I feel these marketing gimmicks are not really gimmicks and are a very faint reality because, for some reason, I have been (mildly) feeling loved. I felt the most love this week when Cotton, my furry friend, and an old boy played and spent time with me for like 20 minutes. This was similar to what Jimmi did, and I wondered if they spoke to each other and conspired.

As I write this, the 2nd farewell to Bettada Hoovu is also complete. The photoshoot farewell. It felt good to have every corner of this abode captured by a good camera and photographer. As days pass, the sinking feeling in my stomach deepens, but I must be fine enough to live every moment here to the fullest.

DAY 107 - 15/2/2025

THE DAY I HAD RAMYUN WITH BETTADA HOOVU

I possibly had the best Valentine's week of my life, and on the day of Valentine's, I spent it eating Thupka at Bettada Hoovu. As I write this, I also had the Ramyun farewell with Bettada Hoovu today, while watching my favourite actor's K-drama. Excitement of the future is still bleak, but at least I have made peace with the present.

Now that the weather has grown warmer, I spend most of my time in the terrace area, feeling bad about why it didn't happen a bit earlier. I smile at my plant, Purple, every morning and tell her that we will be fine, and I hope to be.

I got another bout of deadly flu, and this house was again the only one that checked on me and sheltered me when I was sick. As I write this, I feel much better, and I attribute the healing powers to Bettada Hoovu, and no one and nothing else.

DAY 108 - 16/2/2025

THE DAY I FOUND THE BLACK DOG IN THE DISTANCE

I found the place where the black dog in the distance sits!! It is a government office just a stone's throw from Bettada Hoovu. This is possibly the best closure I could ask for. I had planned on finding him/her and the office he/she sits at, but I never knew this would happen before I left Bettada Hoovu. I planned on greeting the dog, but I found him/her sound asleep and chose to just smile from a distance and come another day.

I also got my bike repaired and serviced, which, as you already know, I regret not caring for well. The smooth and powerful ride it gave me after the service was worth every penny paid for it, and my heart said, "You are now ready to fly."

I had a good time on the terrace today, both morning and evening. I have been making new friends amongst the birds, and my new friend is a bird with a green chest and a black crown (sorry, not too great in ornithology). He/she sits by the terrace grills and sings the most beautiful songs for me. They are so beautiful that often when I see them, I unplug my earphones and listen to his/her songs. Nobody ever has sung a song for me, except my mother's lullabies, and this bird has brought me many smiles just by his/her sheer presence. I also made my personal best paneer curry, with some green peas and black peppers. My heart felt a bit lighter today, and I prayed this would continue.

DAY 109 - 17/2/2025

THE DAY I PLAYED WITH JIMMI AGAIN AND MET A NEW VISITOR

I had a bit of an unpredictable start to the day, as I couldn't get any cabs to go to the office and had to enforce a WFH on myself. Of course, I was happy about it. I made a perfect filter coffee and ate lunch by myself, with gratitude. Last night, I did a bit of star gazing and spotted Jupiter, Mars and Virgo and Cancer constellations. I regretted not doing this earlier, but in my defence, most of the days of my time at Bettada Hoovu, the sky was cloudy.

The chirpy birds have multiplied now, and I wonder if these sounds will ever be replicated in my life again. I also make a mental note that these birds are able to sing so beautifully and visit me because of the tree right in front of Bettada Hoovu, and they will cease to exist once that tree is chopped down. The thought of every tree that has been chopped down in my city for urbanisation gives me shudders. I ogle and sink into the multiple stretches of greenery around Bettada Hoovu and the number of colours they offer in a mere 350 m of stretch. Those who complain and crib about Bangalore traffic have never really counted the number of colours in nature around, I tell myself.

In the evening, while leaving for the gym, I was greeted by a new visitor, Mr. Crow. He was fully jet black and sat like royalty like he owned Bettada Hoovu—I told him he doesn't, and neither do I, which is a very sad reality. On the way back from the gym, I played with Jimmi again, concluding that he was the most affectionate dog in my locality.

After dinner, I walked to the nearby medical shop and purchased some medicines for myself, in my pyjamas and a nightshirt. A privilege I have (had?) in my colony. I come back to Bettada Hoovu and cry a bit, as the inevitable day of shifting houses approaches.

DAY 110 - 19/2/2025

THE DAY I WANTED TO HOLD ONTO TIME

I spent the whole day indoors, including my workout and having a humble yoga session. But I had an amazing day. I captured the sound of the birds, and now that I am left with only 3 nights here (that's less than the time I spent at a place like Dubai, even). The countdown keeps playing in my mind, and time is moving dangerously fast. I am trying to be mindful of every moment, chirp, and ray of sun here. I also frantically googled "How to feel better after losing your prized material possessions and came across some fabulous articles." One of them said something very profound: "Unlike the things you lose, the love you have for them can never be lost, and that's why you never truly lose them".

I promise to this house and myself to always cherish this unique love I have for the house and the version of myself that existed here. I could not have done anything to save this situation, but I tried and lived my best here, and that gave me enough closure to fall asleep tonight.

The part of me that this house gifted to me stays with me. It played its role very well.

All my farewells are now completed, and I am grateful to some very kind and genuine humans who walked with me and felt my grief was valid.

DAY 111 - 20/2/2025

THE DAY I FOUND IMMEASURABLE BEAUTY INSIDE OF ME AND IN THE HOUSE

My penultimate day at Bettada Hoovu. I woke up in the morning, witnessed the sunrise from scratch, and took a video of it. We often take everyday things for granted, and I don't know why this idea dawned on me only today. I also looked around at the spring colours and felt sad that I wouldn't be around to look at the glorious colours around Bettada Hoovu. But this also taught me that just like the spring flowers, our lives are transient too. What we own will fall off one day, and anyway, we take nothing with us. Neither do we bring anything with us to this world.

What rescued me that day was my own life story. I have lived in 11 cities throughout my 30-something years of life, and I carry memories from each of them. Every time I moved cities, it only added to my expanse of life and pool of people I knew and had met. I carry a part of them in me, all of them, and I know their cultures to the core of it, some even better than their locals. That's just me. I loved making a place my home and finding the beauty in it. So I realised that the magic was inside of me, as I was the one who humanised this house and every place I lived in in this beautifully diverse country of India.

This house helped me in so many ways. This book and this chapter won't possibly be enough to share. But until I live and breathe, this house will live through me. A blob of 2 rooms, with just a platform in the name of a kitchen and a terrace area overlooking one of the majestic views in Bangalore, converted into Bettada Hoovu by me. Our life is a book, not a single chapter. And just like all the cities I lived in, this house became an unforgettable, beautiful and memorable chapter for me. However, this chapter differs because it saw the best of me. It saw a version of me I loved most, and I am glad nobody else got to see it but this house. I have no tears as I write this. I just feel acceptance.

When I was writing this chapter, all the people who made this home special for me came trickling down to me. Mr. Kapeesh, how he used to slide the windows and enjoy the sunrise as much as I did, the filter coffee sessions I gifted myself, my maid who was the most frequent visitor to the flat, the eagle gang, the bats' gang, the parrots and tiny birds that sang for me, the sun that rose every single day without fail and made me smile every time, the moon that shone so brightly, the hawkers who would sell flower pots, soppu (meaning leafy vegetables in Kannada), the temple bells, the Hanuman aarti, the dog in the distance, the azaan, Champak, Beasty, Cotton, Jimmi, my plant Purple and so many more. It felt like everyone and everything was now sitting by my side and closing this chapter with nothing but gratitude. And appreciation for any unexpected good things that might happen to all of us. It's funny how I just listed so many things, and I have never felt alone or lonely here.

I would like to end these entries by re-sharing the quote from the book Piranesi, by Sussanna Clarke, which very coincidentally, I read while living here, and nothing describes Bettada Hoovu any better:

"The beauty of the house is immeasurable; its kindness, infinite."

How lucky am I to have lived here, how lucky am I to live here in solitude, how lucky am I to have immortalised this place, how lucky am I to share this with someone as wonderful as you, dear reader. (111)

HANG ON, THIS IS BETTADA HOOVU SPEAKING...

You must be wondering how a house can speak. You're right, they can't, but I can, because I have been breathed into life by this book, the writer, and you, the reader. I was born roughly 5 years ago, and I would say that I was stillborn until the writer came to live here in June 2024. The previous tenants lived here for 3 years, and while they took good care of me, I was always bricks and cement for them. When the writer came here (should I name her? Because she named me too), she saw me beyond 4 walls and 2 blobs of room and the terrace. She thought of a name for me, lived here fully, and documented her life here. I joined her for her filter coffee sessions, when she laughed at K-drama scenes, cried herself to sleep, worked very hard to earn, and when she just did nothing, and so on. I would say the privilege was mine.

Because I cannot think of living here anymore without her, I have decided to join her in her pocket when she shifts into the new home tomorrow. I always want to be her best friend and protector. I will always be there for her and with her. As you humans say, "A friend is one of the best things you can be and the greatest things you can have."

(I am surprised she didn't even realise this when she booked a penthouse again for her next move.)

ACKNOWLEDGEMENTS

This is my first solo publication, and this book would not have been possible without my unemployed phase from January 2024 to April 2024. When you are without what defines most of your life, you learn to truly understand what defines you, which often is never our job or money or titles.

The biggest share of acknowledgement should go to the house I lived in and where this book, including the acknowledgement section, was written. Who knew that a rented house bang in the middle of a commercial area and just parallel to a super busy street would motivate me to write a book so strongly? But such is the beauty of life. When you think it has ended, there comes another reason to carry on. To the locality of Vanganahalli, with those luxury cars, and well-maintained houses where civil people reside (because they mind their own business), and where every human is kind to animals. Those 3 years I could barely find a reason to smile were made so much brighter, thanks to its green canopies, 2 min grocery deliveries, and homely charm. It was a stroke of luck that

I was introduced to this locality and eventually to Bettada Hoovu.

I want to acknowledge 10 people in my acquaintances to whom I sent this idea and who readily, within 5 minutes, encouraged me to write it into a book. That's when this journey began.

I also credit this book to the company I worked for while writing it. I was fortunate to have a manager, team members, leaders, and people around me at work who were always curious about my book and mentioned it very proudly as though it were their own. Not everyone has the privilege of such a workplace and colleagues; I had it while writing this book. I am immensely grateful and appreciative.

Thanking Notion Press for their faith in my work and concept. I still remember when I spoke of my book to the sales consultant, and her immediate reaction of, "wow, I would love to read this!" My day job is very different from book publishing, and Notion Press was kind at every juncture.

To my furry family - Puff, Coffee, Biscuit and Brownie (cat and 3 dogs respectively) - for teaching me what it is to take space in this beautiful world despite being tiny and for living significantly and seeing joy in mundane things like the sunshine, food to eat, and a guaranteed place to sleep.

To my parents for never questioning my dreams. Most times, I just dream and then tell them I want to act on it, and they just nod. In a country where women could get killed for dreaming big, I acknowledge this privilege.

Last but the best, I want to appreciate myself for committing to completing this book and seeing it come to life. I started this book not knowing I would have to leave the house midway, but I still kept going. I kept writing this book even on very busy days, tough days, good days, and every other kind of day.

Your life is very significant, and this world, with all its dark elements, is still absolutely magical. Life happens every day, not only when you marry, have children, get promoted, buy a house, buy a car, etc. So every day is to be thanked for and celebrated. I hope the reader was able to appreciate that about themselves through my story and this book